The Dial

An Historical and Biographical Introduction to Accompany

The Dial

George Willis Cooke

In Two Volumes
Vol. I

NEW YORK
RUSSELL & RUSSELL · INC
1961

L. C. CATALOG CARD NO: 61-13772

PRINTED IN THE U. S. A.

Preface

In this book an attempt has been made to bring together all the accessible facts about the editing and publishing of " The Dial." For many of these facts I have been indebted to other volumes, some of them well known, as in the instance of the biographies of Margaret Fuller, Emerson, and Alcott. Others are rare or but little known, as in the case of Elizabeth Hoar's biography of Mrs. Samuel Ripley, the biography of O. A. Brownson by his son, and many similar works. Other sources of information have been magazines and newspapers, which are to be found in only a few libraries. Many of the facts presented, however, have been obtained at first hand from individuals, by means of interviews and correspondence. I have letters written me by many of the contributors to " The Dial," and these I have frequently quoted or drawn upon for information. Letters from Lowell, Dana, Alcott, Cranch, Ward, Clarke, Cabot, Hedge, Curtis, W. H Channing, Wilson, Miss Peabody, and Miss Clapp, have been thus used.

In the case of those contributors who are well known, the purpose had in view in the following pages has been to state what were their relations to the transcendental club and " The Dial." Those not widely known, or of whom lives have not been published, receive a more detailed biographical treatment. The biographical sketches have not been proportioned according to the extent of the contributions of

the several writers to " The Dial," but rather with reference
to the accessible materials, and the significance of their relations to the transcendental movement. Some of the sketches
would have been longer if the necessary information could
have been secured. In the arrangement of the chapters, the
persons connected with the editing and publishing of " The
Dial " have first received attention, and then the other contributors have been arranged in the order in which their
first contributions appeared.

At the end of the book a full list of all the articles has
been given, with the names of the authors, so far as these
could be ascertained. I am pleased to be able to say that only
four short poems remain anonymous. There follows a second
list, giving in full the contributions of each of the several
authors. In compiling these lists several sources of information have been available. I have been greatly indebted to
Mr. Frank B. Sanborn for information as to the authors, and
for other most important aid. He has in his possession
Thoreau's copy of " The Dial," in which the latter wrote the
names of many of the contributors. As a result of his intimate friendship with Emerson, Thoreau, Alcott, Ellery
Channing, and others, Mr. Sanborn has had abundant opportunities for procuring accurate information. This he has most
generously placed at my disposal. Mr. Alcott also gave me
much aid by means of personal interviews. I have had the
use of Mr. Emerson's set of " The Dial," into which he had
written the names of many of the contributors ; and valuable
information by letter has been given me by Mr. Edward W.
Emerson. Col. T. W. Higginson has also taken a warm interest in my enterprise, and aided me in many ways.
Through the kindness of Dr. Samuel A. Jones, of Ann

Arbor, I have been able to make use of the names written into the set of "The Dial" contained in the library of the University of Michigan. This set was owned by Daniel Ricketson, into which Ellery Channing wrote the names of many of the contributors. I have used the list contained in the Library of Congress, placed there on the authority of Emerson by Dr. Spofford, the former librarian. The list in the Newbery Library of Chicago has been available, as well as that in the Boston Athenæum. The library of Harvard University has also its list, which I have used. Several private sets of "The Dial" have also been consulted, and among them that owned by William S. Robinson ("Warrington"), a native of Concord, and an original subscriber to "The Dial." These lists do not always agree with each other, and it is evident that some of them are more or less based on hearsay, and others are defective because memory is fallible. So far as possible the list given at the end of this book has been revised by the aid of the published works of the several authors. This I have been able to do in the case of Margaret Fuller, Emerson, Thoreau, Cranch, Mrs. Hooper, Parker, and Miss Clapp. Correspondence with Lowell, Clarke, Dana, Curtis, and others, has been used in determining what they wrote. In spite of these precautions, however, a small number of the pieces remain somewhat doubtful as to the authorship.

At one time it was my intention to call this book a history of transcendentalism in New England, but I have thought it better to make use of a less pretentious title. This will account for the first two chapters, in which I have attempted to prove that transcendentalism in New England was essentially indigenous, and that it was a phase of the democratic development in this country. I have been much interested in tracing out the way in which transcendentalism influenced the persons who contributed to "The Dial," and in finding what a leaven of mental purpose it was to most of them, even those the most obscure.

So far as anything in the following pages is concerned, it might be assumed that I am a convinced and unfaltering transcendentalist. The purpose and plan of the book has not made it necessary in any way to discuss the validity of that philosophy, and it is not essential that anything should be said on the subject here. In order to prevent misapprehension, however, I will say that at the present time I am not able to accept the transcendental philosophy. The insight, intuition, or direct contact with the spiritual world, of the transcendentalist, in my opinion, is due to that marvellous process of hereditary and social transmission by which the present is linked to the past. Intuition is the result of that subconscious process of thought by which the individual receives from the past of the race the spiritual issues of its experiences. With this radical qualification, I am not disinclined to accept the teachings of the transcendentalists. They often need a serious criticism, however, in order to free them from excess and fanaticism.

When Frothingham's "New England Transcendentalism" appeared in 1876, I wrote a review of it, which I sent to him. His reply may find a place here, as in some degree expressing my own attitude. "I am happy," he wrote, "to know who wrote the admirable article on transcendentalism and the excellent notice of my book which 'The Spectroscope' [published in Milwaukee] brought me. You have caught the very intent and spirit of my essay, and have

Preface

done full justice to my purpose in writing it. My own position, as somewhere between the two theories — and expectant of new developments — is fairly indicated. I meant to make it appear that, while my faith in the transcendental method was shaken, my faith in the experimental is not confirmed. Transcendentalism has not been refuted. The new sensationalism has not yet been justified. The lover of truth commits himself to no dogma, neither assails nor fanatically defends, but thoughtfully observes. The scientific method must explain everything before it can be acceptable to the highest order of mind. Its success is promising thus far; but as yet, in my judgment, it requires copious supplementing from the spiritual philosophy. This is all I mean by the reference in the preface to myself, and by the criticisms here and there in the text. My apparent noncommittalism is due to my candor in admitting a state of mental — not of spiritual — suspense. The question with me is [one] of bases, not of superstructure. ' The building not made with hands' will endure, though its foundations be of other stone than we fancied."

Psychology has made rapid strides since this letter was written, and a new philosophy, that is at once experiential and transcendental, may now be accepted with confidence. It is to this new psychology, based on the development theory, and tested by a rigid scrutiny of facts, that I commit myself. Whatever its exponents may have to say, it vindicates the better phases of the transcendental philosophy; but on new grounds, and with a truly scientific justification.

GEORGE WILLIS COOKE.

BOSTON, January 7, 1902.

Contents

CHAPTER   PAGE

I. THE BEGINNINGS OF TRANSCENDENTALISM IN AMERICA   1

II. THE FERMENT OF TRANSCENDENTALISM 13

III. THE TRANSCENDENTAL CLUB 40

IV. THE ORIGIN OF THE DIAL 56

V. MARGARET FULLER AS EDITOR OF THE DIAL . . 68

VI. EMERSON AS EDITOR OF THE DIAL 91

VII. THE RIPLEYS 109

VIII. THOREAU AS CONTRIBUTOR AND ASSISTANT EDITOR   117

IX. ELIZABETH PALMER PEABODY 140

X. MEMBERS OF THE TRANSCENDENTAL CLUB . . . 158

XI. CRITICISMS AND CARICATURES OF THE DIAL . . . 170

XII. SUCCESSORS TO THE DIAL 177

Historical and Biographical Introduction to The Dial

I

THE BEGINNINGS OF TRANSCENDENTALISM IN AMERICA

IT has been assumed that transcendentalism had its origin in Germany, and that it was brought here from that country about the year 1830. In a large degree this is true, and yet it has always been indigenous to New England in some form. In the earliest days of Boston it was accepted under the form of antinomianism by John Cotton, Anne Hutchinson, and Sir Henry Vane. By the Friends it was preached with eagerness, and it was nobly exemplified by William Penn in the colony named after him. No one had more of its true spirit than John Woolman, though he taught it only in that form in which it had been promulgated by George Fox. If the Quakers did not largely influence public opinion generally, there were other forces at work to bring it into the currents of religious opinion.

In 1710 there was published in Boston a little book called "The Churches' Quarrel Espoused," in vindication of the congregationalism that had been established in New England. The author was John Wise, minister of Chebacco, in the town of Ipswich; and he wrote in opposition to the proposition of the Mathers that the local parishes should be brought into subjection to associations of churches, which should have the control of their activities in other than merely local interests. Wise put his defence of the churches

1

on the broadest ground of rationality, and showed by his line of argument and his quotations that he had read the idealists to good effect. In his second chapter he says that "reason is congenate with man's nature, wherein by a law immutable, instampt upon his frame, God has provided a rule for men in all their actions, obliging each one to the performance of that which is right, not only as to justice, but likewise as to all other moral virtues, the which is nothing but the dictate of right reason founded in the soul of man." It appears by his book that Wise was not a rationalist, but that the trend of his mind was toward a large idealism, in which he found the grounds of his democratic interpretation of every kind of human government. This idealism appears in his assertion that "the native, internal liberty of man's nature implies a faculty of doing or omitting things according to the direction of his judgment."

That John Wise or any one else in his time had arrived at a definite and consistent assertion of the principles of transcendentalism cannot be claimed; but he and others were looking towards its methods, and acting in accordance with its motives. This may be seen more clearly in what has been called The Great Awakening, that remarkable religious movement which passed over New England about the year 1730, and was first given form by the preaching of Jonathan Edwards. No greater mistake can be made than to suppose that Edwards was a Calvinist strictly of the Puritan type, who called men to a more positive affirmation of the beliefs of the fathers of New England. He it was who first proclaimed the method of conversion as the one by which men might come into full Christian fidelity. That is, he maintained that Christian holiness is an inward and not an outward process, to be secured by direct contact of the soul with God. He was, in a word, an idealist of the most positive religious type, who called men to a life of inward loyalty and purity. The mystic and ideal character of his theology may be best seen in an extract from his diary, written when he was of the age of twenty, concerning Sarah Pierrepont, then only fifteen years old, who subsequently became his wife :

"There is a young lady in New Haven who is beloved of that Great Being who made and rules the world ; and there are certain seasons in which this Great Being, in some way or other invisible, comes to her and fills her mind with exceeding sweet delight, and she hardly cares for anything except to meditate on Him. Therefore, if you present all the world before her, with the richest of its treasures, she disregards it, and cares not for it, and is unmindful of any pain or affliction. She has a strange sweetness in her mind, and a singular purity in her affections ; is most just and conscientious in all her conduct ; and you could not persuade her to do anything wrong or sinful, if you would give her all the world, lest she should offend this Great Being. She will sometimes go about from place to place singing sweetly, and seems to be always full of joy and pleasure, and no one knows for what. She loves to be alone walking in the fields and groves, and seems to have some one invisible always conversing with her."

To the same purport is his account of his meditations on the doxology to the King eternal, immortal, invisible. There then came into his soul, and was, as it were, diffused through it, a sense of the glory of the Divine Being. "I thought with myself," he says, "how excellent a Being that was, and how happy I should be if I might enjoy that God, and be rapt up to Him in heaven, and be swallowed up in Him forever. I kept saying, and, as it were, singing over these words of Scripture, and went to pray to God that I might enjoy Him ; and as I was walking and looking up on the sky and clouds, there came into my mind a sweet sense of the glorious majesty and grace of God. I seemed to see them both in a sweet conjunction : majesty and meekness joined together: it was a sweet, and gentle, and holy majesty, and also a majestic sweetness; an awful sweetness; a high, and great, and holy gentleness."

The stern and forbidding features of Edwards' theology have been those usually recognized, while that side of it seen distinctly in the above extracts has been quite overlooked. Yet he was in no small degree a mystic and an idealist, and it was this element in his religious teaching that gave it power and effectiveness. To a very considerable extent The Great Awakening led to a revival of antinomianism, and this was one of the severest charges brought against it by its opponents. The mystical teachings of this class of the revivalists were widely accepted, and there grew up a considerable body of Separatist churches, which in some degree accepted the doctrines since designated as Perfectionism. In the manner of all idealists and mystics they minimized the outward and ritualistic features of religion, and gave the greatest importance to inward experiences and attitudes of the soul. They held that no outward act of worship could be of value in comparison with the openness of the soul to the mystic influences of God.

The better features of the New Light movement, as it was called, appeared in the theological teachings of Samuel Hopkins. In the true manner of the mystic, Sarah Edwards, in " sweet quietness and alacrity of soul," accepted the right of God to do with her whatever he wished. In the same spirit Hopkins taught the doctrine of an unconditional submission to the will of God, though he proclaimed this surrender in terms which have revolted many tender and sympathetic minds, and caused them to turn against his teachings. It was the idealism of Hopkins, however, that reconciled him to his own doctrines, and that gave him power to teach the law of disinterestedness. More truly than by any other amongst his disciples, the teachings of Edwards were carried forward by Hopkins, and made effective in the growing theology of New England. What that theology was, and what was the effect of the teachings of Hopkins, was stated by William Ellery Channing in a sermon preached by him in Newport, the home of Hopkins throughout all the years of his ministry. "In forming his religious opinions," said Dr. Channing, "he was superior to human authority; he broke away from human creeds; he interpreted God's word for himself; he revered reason, the oracle of God within him. He maintained that all holiness, all moral excellence, consists in benevolence, or disinterested devotion to the greatest good; that this is the character of God; that love is the only principle of the divine administration. . . . True virtue, as he taught, was an entire surrender of personal interest to the benevolent purposes of God. He called us to seek our own happiness as well as that of others in a spirit of impartial benevolence; to do good to ourselves, not from self-preference, not from the impulse of personal desires, but in obedience to that sublime law which requires us to promote the welfare of each and all within our influence. I need not be ashamed to confess the deep impression which this system made on my youthful mind. I am grateful to this stern teacher for turning my thoughts and heart to the claims and majesty of impartial, universal benevolence."

The most idealistic features of the theology of Edwards and Hopkins were accepted by Channing, and he confessed his great indebtedness to them in his student days. They prepared him for the idealism he afterwards found most congenial to his mind. But it was not alone these great theological leaders who found the idealistic conception of the mind the true one, for the minister of the West Church in Boston from 1747 to 1766, Jonathan Mayhew, was of that type of mind. In one of his sermons he said: "Truth is the natural object of reason; an obligation, therefore, to inquire after truth, and to judge what is right, may be found

within us, in our very frame and constitution. This obligation is as universal as reason itself; for every one who is en-
dowed with this faculty is obliged to exercise it in the pursuit
of knowledge, especially of moral and religious knowledge."
Mayhew speaks in other sermons of liberty and active power
in man after a manner to indicate his idealism, as well as
his confidence in them as first-hand manifestations of the
higher power revealed to man. " That we are possessed of
active power," he says, " is so immediately, so experimen-
tally, known by us, and we have such an inward consciousness and feeling of it, that no difficulties merely speculative
can overthrow or in any measure invalidate this evidence of
it." What Mayhew sometimes calls liberty, and sometimes
internal consciousness, he insists upon being of the utmost
importance, the test of revelation, and that without which it
cannot exist. "These are the faculties," he says, " which
the author of our being has given us; nor have we any other
way of coming to the truth which is better than this or even
so sure and infallible. If the truth of these faculties, or the
certainty of the testimony which they bear, is called in
question, we are reduced to a total absolute skepticism, having no data, no first principles, on which to proceed in any
case whatever, whether with reference to religion or common
life."

In the works of such men as John Wise and Jonathan
Mayhew we see the influence of Plato, Plutarch, Cicero, and
other classical writers. Sometimes we find that they have
read Cudworth, More, Law, and other seventeenth-century
mystics and idealists in England. It is quite certain that
throughout the eighteenth century in New England the influence of such men was considerable, even if it was silent
and obscure. It may have been exercised only upon individuals here and there; but it was gradually leading thinking
men away from the older theological positions, and giving a
more inward and a more ideal conception of life. Such

great leaders of religious thought in England as Milton, Til-
lotson, Jeremy Taylor, and Chillingworth were inclined to
idealism ; and they were imbued with the spirit of toleration
and free inquiry. They prepared the way in New England
for that larger soul liberty, as it was called by Roger Wil-
liams and his successors, which in time became the characteristic of its religious life. Perhaps these men did not
know transcendentalism in its fulness of meaning ; but they
one and all, with many others, prepared the way for it and
made its coming certain. Without their work the later developments would have been impossible.

The early English Unitarians were followers of Locke,
and Priestley was a materialist in his philosophy. In this
country Professor Andrews Norton, Dr. Henry Ware, and
others, followed in the same direction. From this philosophy Channing revolted, even as a boy. " The celestial light
of happiness first beamed upon me," he said, " when I was
fifteen years old, in reading Hutcheson's ' Moral Philosophy,'
which makes disinterested benevolence the first principle.
It produced such a boundless flood of joy I could not bear
it." While he was reading this author one day in Cambridge,
as he walked under a clump of willows, he experienced a
remarkable change of spiritual attitude towards the problems
of life. " The place and the hour were always sacred in his
memory," says his biographer, " and he frequently referred
to them with grateful awe. It seemed to him that he then
passed through a new spiritual birth, and entered upon the
day of eternal peace and joy. The glory of Divine disinterestedness, the privilege of existing in a universe of progressive order and beauty, the possibilities of spiritual destiny,
the sublimity of devotedness to the will of Infinite Love,
penetrated his soul."

From this time onward Channing was a believer in the
possibilities of human perfection, that is, that the mind of
man is capable of continuous growth. He ceased to think

of the mind as played upon by outward forces, however high and divine, and came to regard it as having within itself a power very great and efficient. As Hutcheson awakened in him a consciousness of an exhaustless tendency in the human soul to moral perfection, to use his own phraseology, so Ferguson, in his work on Civil Society, gave him the thought of social progress, which was another of his cardinal beliefs. This work aroused in him an enthusiasm for humanity that never deserted him, and that caused him to exclaim that he was "always young for liberty."

While in college Channing also read the works of Richard Price, which, he says, saved him from Locke's philosophy. From Price he obtained the doctrine of ideas; and his " Dissertations " moulded Channing's philosophy into the form it always retained. Throughout life he wrote the words Right, Love, and others of a like nature, with a capital, in order that he might thus express their great importance, as Price had given him to understand and appreciate their significance. Channing was also greatly influenced by Butler in his " Sermons on Human Nature," and by Law in his mystical works. In Butler he found the germs of some of his most important ideas, and Law touched harmoniously many chords of his religious sympathy.

Though none of these writers were distinctly transcendentalists, they were all of them idealists. They refused to accept Locke's dictum that there is nothing in the mind which is not first in the senses, and in one form or another they held that the mind is capable of receiving truth through its own innate activities. This attitude was naturally acceptable to Channing, and any one thoroughly familiar with his works, and his manner of dealing with moral and religious problems, will find it impossible to think of him as holding to any other view. That he was ever in the fullest sense a transcendentalist is not to be claimed, for he was too convinced a believer in the miraculous and the supernatural to accept that philosophy without reserve. He was not wholly emancipated from the beliefs that had been taught in New England from the beginning, and he had no desire to separate himself from what to him was an essential part of Christianity. Nevertheless, he held most firmly to the cardinal principles of idealism; and these were at the foundation of his faith in man and in his continuous progress.

To the innate power in man Channing gave the name of reason, and he said that it belongs to reason to comprehend universal truths. Reason is the power which tends, and is perpetually striving, to reduce our various thoughts to unity or consistency, for it is the most fundamental conviction of reason that all truths agree together. With an unfaltering conviction Channing accepted Christianity as being thoroughly consistent with reason, and as having reason for its chief support and strength. Holding that our rational nature is the greatest gift of God, and that the development of it is the chief end of our being, he declared : "Revelation is but a means, and is designed to concur with nature, providence, and God's spirit, in carrying forward reason to its perfection. I glory in Christianity because it enlarges, invigorates, exalts my rational nature. If I could not be a Christian without ceasing to be rational, I should not hesitate as to my choice. I feel myself bound to sacrifice to Christianity property, reputation, life; but I ought not to sacrifice to any religion that reason which lifts me above the brute and constitutes me a man. I can conceive no sacrilege greater than to prostrate or renounce the highest faculty which we have derived from God. In so doing we should offer violence to the divinity within us."

It will be seen that Dr. Channing was essentially a transcendentalist; and it was inevitable he should be often regarded as the founder of the movement in New England which took that name. He may not have accepted all that was put forth as transcendentalism, but its cardinal ideas were his ; and his religious teachings were in harmony with its spirit. Elizabeth Peabody rightly said that in the transcendental movement she knew no older name than Dr. Channing's. She says that, so early as 1820, he began to emancipate her mind from the materialistic teachings of Priestley ; and from him she first learned the meaning of the word " transcendental," when he introduced her to a knowledge of Coleridge. It was to Coleridge that Channing owed much of his own spiritual philosophy; and he was very little, if at all, indebted to Kant and the later German thinkers. Frothingham says that Channing was a transcendentalist in sentiment, but not in thought; but this is a distinction which his own quotations refute. That Channing repelled many of the extravagances of the transcendentalists does not take him out of their company or make it less certain that his manner of thinking was their own.

Col. T. W. Higginson says that transcendentalism in New England had at least one merit, that it was indigenous. This is the simple truth about it, that it was a part of the growing individualism that marked the development of democracy. Some of its later phases were undoubtedly due to the influence of Coleridge, Kant, and Cousin ; but it had a life of its own long before, and gave itself many forms of utterance. It might be difficult to give chapter and verse to authenticate its presence in positive statements of philosophical opinion, but it pervaded the whole of New England life, and was especially marked in its religious changes. There was a direct descent of this line of thinking from Edwards, through Hopkins and Channing, to Emerson. Each of these men was largely influenced by his predecessor, not as to the whole of his theological system, but in the one direction of the growth of idealism. Each acknowledged in generous words his debt to his predecessor, and attributed to him the growth of his own mind in the direction which was most characteristic of his matured thinking. If each advanced far beyond his master, it was along the line of what was most original in his thought and most worthy of greater development.

Nothing is more certain than that Emerson's transcendentalism was native to his mind, not borrowed from any master he may have followed, or gained from any foreign importation. It had been in the life and thought of his family for generations, and if in him it first came to a positive expression of sufficient force to gain it wide public recognition, it did not begin with him. Two prize essays written by him when he was an undergraduate in Harvard College, and when he could have known nothing about German philosophy, prove that he was already a transcendentalist. In his essay on " The Present State of Ethical Philosophy," for which he won the Bowdoin prize in 1821, at the age of eighteen, he said of moral science : " It was the beautiful and eternal offspring of other worlds, and conferred on this by interposition which no discoveries might anticipate." He says that the moral faculty " is recognized as an original principle of our nature, — an intuition by which we directly determine the merit or demerit of action." This statement he makes more emphatic when he says : " Every discussion of this science carries with it this recommendation, that it is a new assertion of the highest human privileges." Again : " Morality is constituted the rule by which the world must stand. The laws which govern society are only compends, more or less imperfect, of natural morality."

This was but a crude and youthful statement of the principles held by the transcendentalists ; but the essence of them was here, and distinctly apprehended. It was only necessary that they should be carried to their logical results to give us the teachings we find in Emerson's " Nature " and

11

in his early addresses. But in the meantime his ideas were taking shape, and early in 1826, when he was but twenty-three years old, in writing to his aunt of his beginning soon to preach, he said : " There are in each man's history insignificant passages which he feels to be, to him, not insignificant; little coincidences in little things, which touch all the springs of wonder, and startle the sleeper, Conscience, in the deepest cell. The mind stands forth in alarm, with all her faculties suspicious of a Presence which it behooves her deeply to respect; touched not more with awe than with curiosity, if perhaps some secret revelation is not about to be vouchsafed, or doubtful if some moral epoch is not just now fulfilled in its history — and the tocsin just now struck that tolls out an irreparable past." This expression of transcendentalism was made more emphatic in a letter written a year later, soon after he had begun preaching. "Every man is a new creation," he says, "can do something best; has some intellectual modes and forms, or a character the general result of all, such as no other agent in the universe has."

With this essential transcendentalism Emerson began his intellectual life. It had been taught him by his mother, and his aunt, Mary Moody Emerson, and in the preaching of Dr. Channing. He needed to go to no more remote teacher for its spirit and its intent. After he had left the pulpit Emerson gave an even more explicit utterance to the faith that had been his from his early years, when he said : " I believe I am more of a Quaker than anything else. I believe in the still small voice; and that voice is Christ within us." This native idealism of his mind makes it impossible to think of him as at any time other than a transcendentalist. This tendency drew him to Coleridge, Carlyle, and the German thinkers; but he went to them because he had long before found his way to that manner of thinking which was theirs.

II

THE FERMENT OF TRANSCENDENTALISM

IT is a mistake to suppose that the transcendental movement was merely philosophical and religious. It was more
truly moral and practical, aiming at social reforms and the
enlargement of the sphere of education. An undue emphasis has been placed upon its philosophical aspects by Frothingham and others, the result of the attempt to show that
it had its origin in Germany. Against this conclusion
almost every original transcendentalist has protested; and
they were fully justified in so doing by the facts. Writing
to Carlyle, in October, 1840, Emerson said: "We are all a
little wild here with numberless projects of social reform.
Not a reading man but has a draft of a new Community in
his waistcoat pocket. I am gently mad, and am resolved
to live cleanly. One man renounces the use of animal
food; and another of coin; and another of domestic hired
service; and another of the State; and on the whole we
have a commendable share of reason and hope." In fact,
the chief characteristic of this movement was its eagerness
for what is fresh, natural, and human. It has been truly
called the "Newness," for the transcendentalists can be
designated as a party or a sect only in the sense that they
desired a new world, to get rid of the old, and to start
afresh with all things.

The transcendentalist forgot the past or ignored it, and
was of the opinion that it was but necessary to think out
what was reasonable and just in order to realize it as a fact.
He was not always a follower of Rousseau; but he desired
what was instinctive, primitive, aboriginal, what belonged

to the nature of man as a moral being. He was, therefore, ready to cast aside convention and custom, and to seek for what is ideally and theoretically right. This attitude made him a reformer; and he was not contented until he had overturned that which is venerable, and put what is youthful and rational in its place. His purpose was of the noblest; but his means were sometimes wholly inadequate to the reforms he sought to accomplish, and his methods were too often revolutionary and iconoclastic. That he accomplished much good cannot be doubted, and yet the results in the direction of getting rid of the evils of society were small indeed in comparison with what his theories demanded. The whole movement was a ferment, a stirring of the deep waters of social placidity, resulting in a great increase of discussion and criticism.

All this was incidental to the growth of democracy, and to the youthful expression of that spirit which had given life to the Republic. The first half of the last century brought out the nature of individualism as it has been never before in the history of the world, and perhaps more fully in New England than anywhere else. Personal freedom and the liberty of individual opinion and conduct was the demand of all vigorous men and women. Not to be guided by the conduct of others was the right claimed by many persons. They broke away, therefore, from the old beliefs, the age-long customs, the consecrated ideals, and the moral maxims of other days. They wished to act for themselves, and they were ready to accept the consequences of their conduct. They were not irreligious, but they were no longer willing to accept the religion of the fathers. They were not irreverent, but they would not obey the commands of those great ones who had lived long ago.

On its religious side transcendentalism found its first expression in the Unitarian protest. That protest was essentially moral in its nature, being a revolt from conceptions of

God and man that were not democratic in their origin and nature. When the democratic idea had taken hold sufficiently of the people to realize itself in morals and religion, it led to a revolt against the monarchical conception of God, and the autocratic ideal of human nature. The result was the Unitarian, Universalist, Christian, Swedenborgian, liberal Orthodox, broad church, and many other phases of the religious assertion of the equality of all men, and of the human nature of God. The Puritanic assertion of the "sovereignty" of God was no longer acceptable, because "the divine right of the king" had no meaning in a republic. Whether this way of thinking was theologically correct or not, it had a very great influence upon the religious attitude of men who were fully realizing that they were citizens of a democratic nation.

The Unitarian movement was ethical rather than theological. If all men are free and equal, and every man has a right to assert his individuality as one of the rulers of the nation, then every man also has the right to think his own thoughts about God, and to liberty of religious belief. Individuality in politics naturally led to individuality in religion. If it is right to assume that every man is competent to take part in the government, it followed almost inevitably that many men said that every man has reason enough to make his own religion. The Unitarian movement held in itself the germs of the transcendentalism that followed. It is true that many Unitarians rejected with scorn and contempt the teachings of the transcendentalists, but that was because they did not advance to the logical results of their own doctrines. The real leaders of Unitarianism, those who have made it what it is in this country to-day, such men as Channing, Emerson, Walker, Francis, Hedge, Clarke, Parker, and many others, were transcendentalists in the sense of being open-minded, progressive, and rational. They were evolutionists before the development theory had been announced; and they maintained that religion must be vital with movement and advance.

At first transcendentalism was but a phase of the Unitarian movement; but it gradually found its manifestation in most Protestant sects, and in the creation of new religious bodies. Almost without exception the writers for " The Dial" were Unitarians. Some of them, as in the instance of Thomas T. Stone and William B. Greene, became Unitarians because of their interest in the transcendental movement. There were others, however, who gradually worked their way out of Unitarianism, — O. A. Brownson, Mrs. George Ripley, and others, found their way into the Roman Catholic Church, while William D. Wilson and J. T. Tuckerman became Episcopalians. There may have been other changes, but these are indicative of them all. It is also to be recognized that transcendentalism was a strong ferment within Unitarianism itself, and lead to the long and bitter controversy with Theodore Parker, to the organization of the Free Religious Association, and to theological discussions that lasted for half a century.

Unitarianism was only one phase of the religious ferment of the time, and of not less interest is that tendency which drew many of the transcendentalists to the study of Swedenborg. Almost without exception the "newness" men and women turned to the Swedish seer as to one of their own kind, worthy to receive recognition with Kant, Schelling, Coleridge, and Channing. Emerson read Swedenborg with interest, Parker turned to him with curiosity, and Henry James the elder became in a measure a disciple. At Brook Farm Swedenborg was much read or, at least, much discussed; and there was found a close affinity between his teachings and those of Fourier. In " The Harbinger" these two were often referred to as teaching the same doctrines, as leading to the same conceptions of life and social action. Warren Burton, one of the earliest members of the Brook

Farm Association and a Unitarian minister, is said to have accepted the teachings of Swedenborg; but this could have been said to a greater or less extent of many others. Sampson Reed, of Boston, who often came into close association with the transcendentalists, was a devoted adherent of the New Church and its teachings. C. J. Hemple wrote a book, published in this country, on the extraordinary resemblances between the views of Fourier and Swedenborg. In " The Present " W. H. Channing published several articles on the subject, it being a favorite one with him. While Swedenborg had a marked influence on the transcendentalists, partly in the way of protest, as well as in that of affirmation, few of them were drawn in any large degree to the religious body that represents his teachings. It was in a large way he influenced them, through the vast suggestiveness of his ideas, and especially by means of his doctrine of the correspondence between the material world and that of spiritual realities.

Col. T. W. Higginson has shown us that there was a movement of religious protest and idealism not influenced in any degree by the men whose names are usually cited as representing transcendentalism. It was a people's movement, that had its origin amongst farmers, fishermen, and factory operatives. Such movements appeared in the form of Universalism, and in that body of believers which would accept no other name than Christian; but the Come-Outers were of nearer kin to the transcendentalists. It was thoroughly a democratic movement, an uprising and protest of the common people, moved to declare that religion is a matter of life and duty, and not one of priests and churches. Higginson describes the Come-Outer element as " being fearless, disinterested, and always self-asserting. It was abundant on Cape Cod, and the Cape-Codders were a recognized subdivision at reform meetings. In such meetings or conventions these untaught disciples were often a source of

obvious inconvenience; they defied chairmen, scaled plat-
forms, out-roared exhorters. Some of them, as Emerson
says, devoted themselves to the worrying of clergymen;
proclaiming a gospel of freedom, I have heard them boast of
having ascended pulpits and trampled across their cushions
before horrified ministers. This was not a protest against
religion, for they were rarely professed atheists, but against
its perversions alone."

In August, 1840, Parker, Ripley, Cranch, and others,
attended a Come-Outer convention at Groton; and Parker
wrote in his diary of two of their ministers from Cape Cod,
that " they were as rough-looking men as you would find in
a summer's day, — rough, I mean, in their exterior, for their
countenance was full of the divine. Their hands, their
dress, their general air, showed they belonged to the hum-
blest class in society." He found that these men gave little
esteem to the ordinances of the church, though they did not
wholly discard them, that they accepted as members of their
societies any who chose to meet with them, that their
preachers were generally illiterate and earned their living
by other occupations, that they accepted the Bible with
reserve, fearing to worship it. They said that " the Bible is
a scripture of the Word, not the Word itself; for the Word
is never written save in the living heart." It will be seen
that these people had some resemblances to the early Quakers,
while they developed relations to the Adventists and Perfectionists of our own day. They agreed with the transcendentalists in insisting that religion is not a form or a ritual,
but an inward life; and that the communications of the
Spirit are not through a book or a church, but directly to
the soul.

The Come-Outers appeared in many parts of New England, and were the result of the slowness of the churches
in accepting the reforms of the day, especially anti-slavery.
Their churches did not continue in existence more than a

few years, and by the time of the Civil War they had disappeared from recognition by the name that had been given them by their enemies. There were a number of churches, however, that withdrew from denominational alliance, owing to their anti-slavery convictions; and a smaller number were organized distinctly on that basis. This was but a small influence at the largest, but nearly all denominations were more or less deeply moved by this ferment. Not distinctly as a part of it, and yet caused by somewhat the same stirrings of the mind and heart, was the Adventist movement. This was the form in which many persons in New England at this time declared their faith in a new heaven and a new earth. As a phase of this religious development, or as one parallel with it, was the revival of Antinomianism known as Perfectionism, which found expression in most of the evangelical churches. The Adventists were dissatisfied with life as they found it, and looked to the immediate coming of Christ in order that the world might be reformed, while the Perfectionists insisted that it is possible for the individual believer to reach such a degree of faith as to be without sin. As a rule the Perfectionists accepted the doctrine of the second-coming, while the Adventists were almost without exception believers in perfectionism. Therefore, we have here another phase of transcendentalism, or an idealism determined as to its nature and outward expression by an immediate and vital faith in Christ.

An interest in transcendentalism was by no means absent from the more strictly orthodox believers in the evangelical churches. One phase of this interest may be seen in the books of Thomas C. Upham, professor of mental and moral philosophy in Bowdoin College. His text-books of mental philosophy were once largely used in American colleges, and this fact indicates that a phase of transcendentalism was widely acceptable in evangelical churches.

Upham was one of the leaders of the Perfectionist movement, but he had also a strong affinity for what in Europe
has been called Quietism. This form of mysticism is essentially the same as transcendentalism, though it more distinctly accepts the beliefs and rituals of orthodoxy. Upham
wrote a biography of Madame Guyon, as well as of Madame
Catharine Adorna; and the teachings of such Catholics
as Fénelon he accepted with zeal and admiration. His own
teachings were elaborated in the "Principles of the Interior
or Hidden Life," which was reviewed in the last volume of
"The Dial" by Charles Lane.

The approval given to Upham's work by Lane shows
clearly enough how closely allied this phase of Perfectionism was to transcendentalism. Upham says in this book
that a form of religious experience that may be denominated the interior or hidden life "indicates a greatly advanced state of religious feeling, resulting in a sacred and
intimate union with the Infinite Mind." What he thus
defines differs from transcendentalism only in its peculiarly
religious form, and not at all in its philosophical foundation.
Upham's presentation of mysticism has less of individualism
in it than characterizes transcendentalism, and he taught
that the soul should become entirely submissive to the will
of God in the Quietist manner. " Man never acts to higher
and nobler purpose," he says, " that when, in the realization
of his own comparative nihility, he places himself in the
receptive position, and lets God work in him. In the intercourse between man and his Maker, it is the receptive and
not the communicative activity, which is the source of truth
and power."

The transcendentalist maintained that God comes into
the soul through the natural processes of its normal activity,
but the Quietist said it was through the entire abnegation
of self. Upham held to a supernatural process as taking
place in the soul, which the transcendentalist denied, claim-

ing that it was entirely natural and normal. Whoever accepts the Christian faith, however, as set forth by Upham, comes into the same kind of inward union with God that the transcendentalist accepted as his cardinal philosophical tenet. We find Upham describing this process as "inward recollection," which he defines as "that serious and collected state of mind in which God is realized and felt as the inward and present counsellor, guide, and judge of all actions, both internal and external." He again says : " The principle is that of inward quietude or stillness; in other words, a true and practical ceasing from self." Describing the effects of this quietude, he says : "To talk with God — to go to him familiarly as children to a parent — to speak to him in the secrecy of their spirits, and to receive an inward answer as gracious as it is decisive, is not only a privilege granted them, but a privilege practically realized. We think it impossible for a person to be truly and wholly the Lord's without frequently being the subject of this inward and divine intercourse."

No argument is needed to prove that Quietism and Perfectionism are not transcendentalism; but that they have close relations to each other the history of both religion and philosophy amply prove. What is here maintained is that, while transcendentalism found a large place amongst the Unitarians and others of a liberal turn of mind, Perfectionism was having a like development, and from much the same causes, amongst those evangelical in belief. Nor was transcendentalism wholly absent from amongst the orthodox, as may be seen in the interest that James Marsh, president of the University of Vermont, took in the writings of Coleridge. In 1829 Marsh edited the " Aids to Reflection " from the first English edition, prefacing it with a long expository essay, and adding numerous notes. In 1831 he edited "The Friend" with enthusiastic approval. Both these volumes were published in Burlington, and they seem to have had a considerable sale. In the preface to the second of these works Marsh said of the first, that when it was published "there were many occasions of doubt with regard to its probable reception. These doubts are now removed. The result has justified the most flattering anticipations, and furnishes abundant proof that the fit audience to be found among us for works of this kind is not so small as had been apprehended. Indeed, the manner in which that work has been received, the sentiments which it has awakened, and the class of persons whose attention has been specially directed to it, are such as furnish the best security for the success of similar works in future."

This testimony is sufficient to cause us to think that transcendentalism did not arise in this country in a little Boston coterie, and that it was not an importation from Germany. In his preface to the "Aids to Reflection," which preceded in its date of publication any book by those who are usually known as transcendentalists, Marsh says of Coleridge, that "he boldly asserts the reality of something distinctly spiritual in man, and the futility of all those modes of philosophizing in which this is not recognized or which are incompatible with it." This conclusion he accepts and loyally defends, but he says this theory may be "denominated a philosophical statement and vindication of the distinctively spiritual and peculiar doctrines of the Christian system." This was what Coleridge had maintained, and Marsh is careful to assert that this philosophy is in distinct opposition to that which was generally accepted at the time in this country. When Marsh says that the "Christian faith is the perfection of human reason," he declares what Theodore Parker at a later date made one of the cardinal tenets of his preaching in Boston. "There is, and can be, in this highest sense of the word, but one reason," says Marsh, "and whatever contradicts

22

that reason, being seen to do so, cannot be received as matter either of knowledge or faith." That Marsh was essentially in sympathy with the teachings of the later transcendentalists may be seen in such a passage as this from his essay : "It is a fact of great importance to be kept in mind that in the study of ourselves, in attaining a knowledge of our own being there are truths of vast concernment, and living at a great depth, which yet no man can draw for another. However the depth may have been fathomed, and the same truth brought up by others, for a light and a joy to their own minds, it must still remain, and be sought for by us, each for himself, at the bottom of the well." Here Marsh recognizes the principle of individuality, which Upham seems to have ignored ; and without that transcendentalism does not come to its full expression.

In the short article on " Transcendentalism " prepared by Emerson for the Editor's Table of " The Dial" for January, 1842, there is published a letter from Thomas T. Stone, who is mentioned as "the Calvinist." In this letter Stone maintains that " all the peculiarities of the theology denominated Trinitarian are directly or indirectly transcendental." He proceeds briefly to give his reasons for this statement : " The sinfulness of man involves the supposition of a nature in man which transcends all limits of animal life and of social moralities. The reality of spirit, in the highest sense of that holy word, as the essence of God, and the inward ground and law of man's being and doing, is supposed both in the fact of sin, and the possibility of redemption from sin. The mystery of the Father revealed only in the Son as the Word of Life, the Light which illumines every man, outwardly in the incarnation and offering for sin, inwardly as the Christ in us, energetic and quickening in the inspirations of the Holy Spirit, — the great mystery wherein we find redemption, — this, like the rest, is transcendental." Then he proceeds to say that the Trinitarians are not faithful to this side of their own beliefs, that they prefer what is "empiric, sensuous, inductive." He condemns the philosophy generally accepted by evangelical Christians quite in the same spirit as that shown by Dr. Marsh in his introduction to Coleridge's "Aids to Reflection." He says that "a system which used to create and sustain the most fervid enthusiasm, — as is its nature, for it makes God all in all, — leads in crusade against all, even the purest and gentlest, enthusiasm." What is of most interest in this short article, however, are the few words at its opening, in which Emerson plainly recognizes the universality of the religious sentiment, and of that spiritual philosophy which sustains it. Called by many names, there is a perfect identity in its essential nature, whatever the form it takes from time to time.

Dissatisfaction with the present conditions of life, and faith in a better world as possible, characterized all the phases of the religious ferment of this period. What united them together was their common idealism, their confidence that a change in the inward life was capable of bringing about the reform in human living they desired. It was not by a better government, a truer organization of society, a common sharing of property, that these persons hoped to secure a truer kind of living ; but by an inward reformation, a closer union of the soul with Christ or with God.

It is not to be assumed, however, that the majority went over to the acceptance of these distinctly idealistic conceptions of how the world was to be reformed. Sharing with them fully in their dreams of a reformed world, was a class that looked to more material means to that end. Those who joined in the Brook Farm Association, and the kindred experiments at Hopedale and Northampton, as well as in many other parts of the country, believed in the use of practical means in bringing about the desired reformation. These persons said that it was essential the environment should be

improved as well as the heart transformed. There was,
therefore, a radical difference between the two classes, not
only as to the means used, but as to the philosophy of
human improvement. While Emerson and Thoreau, Ripley
and Hedge, are alike classed as transcendentalists, they differed vitally from each other as to the method by which
reform was to be secured. Emerson and Thoreau were
individualists, and maintained that all social progress is to
come through the individual and the inward rightness of his
life. On the other hand, Ripley and Hedge were socialists,
in that they believed that reformation is to be brought about
by social effort. Ripley agreed with many others in believing that a new organization of society is essential, that shall
be altruistic, co-operative, and mutually helpful. Hedge
was not so much interested in this method of reform as in
that social effort which is inherited from the past of the
organized church and institutional religion. While Emerson and Thoreau were uncompromising individualists, and
would not give their adhesion to Brook Farm or Fruitlands,
or to any associative method of reforming society, yet they
did not stand wholly aloof from the reforms of their day.
Emerson freely criticised the reformers, and insisted that
what was needed did not consist in petty social changes, but
in the inward reformation of individuals. How can a man
reform others until he has first made himself right? was his
constant inquiry. On the other hand, such men as Ripley,
W. H. Channing, and Adin Ballou, were not the less transcendentalists because they did not accept Emerson's uncompromising individualism. They criticised Emerson for his
coldness, his aloofness from social effort, his self-sufficiency
and hauteur of manner. They said he did not realize the
worth of altruism, that he did not appreciate the real value
of associative movements. Unquestionably, Emerson was
not so much of a reformer as he would have been had he
been less of an individualist. It is to be recognized, how-

ever, that all the transcendentalists, whether individualists or associationists, were committed to the great radical reform of their time, that for the widest extension of human liberty. Every transcendentalist was in greater or lesser degree a worker in the anti-slavery movement. Channing and Emerson have been freely and severely criticised for their slowness in associating themselves with the anti-slavery movement, and for their half-heartedness in its promotion ; but it must be understood that these men were not of the rough and ready kind that make the best reformers, that they were not iconoclasts, that they could not accept the methods used by many of the promoters of reform. They were not essentially men of action, but men of ideas. And they saw the difficulties of the task to be accomplished as was not done by the more urgent reformers, and how many conflicting interests were involved. Hence their slowness, which made them steadfast and immovable when once they had committed themselves to the cause of freedom. However, there was never any hesitation with them as to the nature and necessity of freedom, only as to the methods to be employed in securing it to the enslaved. We can now see that their hesitation was justified, for liberty and the ballot have not given the hitherto slaves the freedom that was desired for them, even after the gigantic sacrifice the nation made to secure it.

This is to be recognized, that the New England transcendentalists were not closet philosophers or those concerned only with an inward as opposed to an outward religion. While this movement was largely ethical and religious, it was also practical ; and it concerned itself with the realities of every-day life. Because of the predominance of Emerson's genius, which was distinctly inward and idealistic, the practical efforts of the transcendentalists have been overlooked. In fact, they were much concerned with the outward reformation of religion. Even Emerson, individualist

that he was, and scornful as he was towards all efforts at
the betterment of life by aid of external appliances, did not
by any means hold himself aloof wholly from the attempt
to secure a more genuine Christianity for New England.
His paper on the Chardon Street and Bible Conventions,
published in the third volume of "The Dial," shows how
great was his interest in genuine attempts to bring religion
and daily life into harmony with each other. These meetings, continued for two or three years, beginning in 1840, were
one phase of the Come-Outer movement, and had the same
objects in view. One of the subjects discussed was the
keeping of the Sabbath in a rational manner, so that it
might become a real means of social and individual betterment. Another was the reformation of the church, in order
to bring it more fully into harmony with modern needs.
There was undoubtedly a strongly felt iconoclastic spirit
manifest in these meetings towards organized religion, but
which sought its reformation, and not its destruction.
There was also a free handling of the Bible, that often
seemed truly infidel in its nature and purposes, but that
really desired to give the Bible to the people as an open
book, not as a fetish. What these men and women aimed
at was to open the interior of the Bible, to give it power as a
source of spiritual strength, to make it a light within. In
describing these conventions, Emerson defined the true
nature of transcendentalism, as it sought for reformation of
the ethical life, the social methods, and the religious spirit
of mankind. "These men and women," he wrote, "were in
search of something more satisfying than a vote or a defini-
tion, and they found what they sought, or the pledge of it,
in the attitude taken by individuals of their number, of resistance to the insane routine of parliamentary usage, in the
lofty reliance on principles, and the prophetic dignity and
transfiguration which accompanies, even amidst opposition
and ridicule, a man whose mind is made up to obey the

great inward Commander, and who does not anticipate his own action, but awaits confidently the new emergency for the new counsel."

These idealists were intensely practical in their aims, at least in regard to the methods by which they sought to secure the results of their idealism. If they sought for inward reformation, they were not less eager to bring about an outward transformation of the individual and of society. This was the time of the bloomer costume, the use of Graham bread, the frequent application of cold water, the abandonment of strong drink, the refusal to use animal food, and the acceptance of the principle of non-resistance. Scornful as Emerson was towards such reforms as these, that put infinite stress upon a cleanly outward life, and left the soul a prey to doubt and discontent, they were a remarkable phase of the life of the time. A reformed dietetics, and a new and more rigid asceticism, were no necessary part of the transcendental movement; and yet they were closely allied with it. The new idealists accepted many of these reforms as a legitimate consequence of their transcendentalism; and some of them attempted to practically realize them all in their own individual conduct. What was called the " Sisterhood of Reforms " was accepted by nearly all the transcendentalists; and it is by no means true that Emerson kept himself aloof from them, however keen the sting of his shafts hurled at them in his lectures. He was as much committed to them as was possible to a person whose mind worked as did his, not dogmatically, but with desire to weigh all facts and to accept only what is inwardly realizable.

It was in this time of ferment that women began to come out of their seclusion and to take part in the activities of reform. This was but a phase of the individualism of the time, and it demanded for woman the same right to be herself that man was seeking for himself. It was, in fact, a refusal to accept the domination of conventionalism, and an assertion that the individual should rely on his own genius. If men have a right to claim their true individuality, why have not women the same right? If all men are free and equal, why not all women? The woman movement was the democratic movement realizing itself logically, demanding for women what it had accepted for men. It was no mere coincidence that Margaret Fuller, the leader in the woman movement, was also one of the most devoted of the transcendentalists. Almost without exception the idealists were in favor of freedom for women; and the women who came forward as the leaders of their sex were transcendentalists or inclined to that philosophy of life. This could not have been otherwise, for the transcendentalists were individualists, asserting for the soul the inward source of social power and rule, that must have for women the same meaning as for men. It was this assertion of individuality, without which transcendentalism would have had no meaning, that led Margaret Fuller to say, in the first article in the fourth volume of "The Dial," that "men do *not* look on both sides, and women must leave off asking them and being influenced by them, but retire within themselves, and explore the groundwork of being till they find their peculiar secret." This assertion of individuality has given to women a larger recognition before the law, and greatly increased opportunities for education. It has also brought about some agitation as to marriage, and personal rights therein; but it has elevated the sex, and made social life freer and truer. If individuality has any such meaning as the transcendentalists gave it, either theoretically or practically, then it is evident that women are to realize themselves most truly as human beings, not by being the echoes of men, but by asserting their own peculiar personal power.

In the transcendental club women were for the first time in America put upon a footing of perfect intellectual equality with men. Not one of its members questioned the right of Margaret Fuller, Elizabeth Peabody, or Sarah Ripley to take part in its discussions, and they were accorded the same opportunities and the same courtesies as the other members. When the Town and Country Club, however, lived its brief day, and members came into it actuated by the usual conventional motives, women were refused recognition. What this movement meant as to women was not that they are always and everywhere the equals of men; but that their individuality is as essential as that of men, and that they should be accorded the same right to be themselves as women that men have to be themselves as men.

Another phase of the ferment of the time was the desire for the improvement of the working-men and their families. A working-men's party was formed in Philadelphia in 1827, and for some years it maintained an organization. It was not as a political movement, however, that the cause of labor was most effectively promoted, but rather in connection with education and general enlightenment. In some degree the laborers became class conscious, but with no thought of emancipating themselves from the rest of the community. To make labor dignified was a part of the gospel of the time, and it did not seek to oppose class to class, but to make labor universal, and therefore respectable. Not only was the working-man to be educated, and to share in the intellectual movement of the time, but the man of culture was to turn laborer for the sake of a more robust manhood and a sounder education. Societies were organized to promote the interests of labor, newspapers were published in every larger city in that behalf, and many a pulpit and platform glorified the cause of the laborer and preached the high dignity of toil. Great meetings of working-men were held in New York and elsewhere to aid in redeeming manual labor from its servile condition. One newspaper advocated that all estates, on the death of their owners, should revert to the State, that they might then be portioned out to the young men and women who were in need of them in entering upon their life work. O. A. Brownson advocated something very near socialism and the equalization of opportunities, though he refused to accept the socialistic scheme as his own.

A most interesting phase of the labor reform movement was that which expressed itself in efforts of the women operatives in Lowell to improve their condition. These young women from New England farms organized clubs for intellectual improvement, listened to courses of lectures, and published and edited a magazine of much intellectual ability. "The Lowell Offering" was a work of real merit, considering the fact that its editors and writers were mill operatives; and it was widely read and praised. Among its writers were Lucy Larcom, Harriot F. Curtis, Harriet Farley, and others, who gained for themselves a reputation as writers, and Margaret F. Foley, who became an artist of considerable ability. Harriet J. Hanson (Mrs. Robinson), one of "the mill-girls," has written the history of this most interesting phase of early factory life; and her other books have given her recognition as an author. "The Dial" was read by these young women, and the Brook Farm experiment was discussed by them. They came from the farms and villages of northern New England, and they nobly represented the inquisitive and studious life of the time. They were intelligent, eager for an education, improved every opportunity to enlarge their knowledge, and have been most useful members of society. Perhaps no better representative of the intellectual influences of the time could be selected than the mill girl, because of her educational and literary efforts. She was truly typical of the eagerness of the people for a higher intellectual and spiritual life, breaking over the old conventional barriers, and laboring in a simple manner for the real successes of life. These operatives came from excellent families, often had as good a pedigree as any one in New England; and they frequently advanced to the best positions in society.

It was with such persons the labor movement began; and in its early days, at least, it gained in power and dignity through their wise leadership.

Writing to O. A. Brownson, December 18, 1842, George Ripley said of the Brook Farm enterprise: " I consider it as the incarnation of those transcendental truths which we have held in common, and which you have done much to make me love. To perceive the worth of man as man, to see through the hollowness and injustice of our social conventionalities, and to resolve on the reform of my own household, were with me almost simultaneous acts. This resolve attracted kindred spirits, and here we are. This is the *mot d'énigme* of all our movement. How can I feel but gratified in seeing lofty practical visions embodied in the most truly democratic state that I have ever known — small as may be the ground plan of our edifice. You know the keen enjoyment I took in the discussions of the most abstract theories; these theories, however, all bore on the possible future of humanity; and now, in living them, shall I confess there is an inward delight, such as one would scarce dream of, — so great as to produce a disinclination either to speak or write about them, — so much more intense is the daily consciousness of life ? With the vivid feeling that the great revolution in my life plan was the inevitable fruit of the ideas for which you most valued me, I will own to something of disappointment that you should give us so little sympathy or recognition, when a friendly word would have been cheering amidst such a tempest of abuse as fell upon us from the conservative sky. . . . As to your questions, it is true that some of our young people are not quite free from nonsense. They unconsciously worship R. W. E. with a too blind adoration, and like that master, express themselves confusedly. They are pure, simple souls, apparently without an erring instinct, and their beautiful divine lives would seem to sanction their doctrine."

This letter indicates with unquestionable directness how closely Brook Farm was associated with the transcendental movement. Not all the associative organizations of the time were so nearly related to it, but such was the case with all those in New England. In a more direct way than with any other, Brook Farm grew out of transcendentalism; and during the first three or four years of its existence it was the visible representative of the motives and ideals of that form of thought. After Dr. Channing, Emerson was the first person consulted by Ripley when he was planning this association; but Emerson was too much an individualist to commit himself to such a form of social combination. However, he was keenly interested in the attempt thus made, and was an occasional visitor. As Ripley indicates, Emerson had a deep influence upon the persons who formed the Brook Farm community, and his teachings were received with reverence. Not only Ripley, but Dwight, W. H. Channing, Margaret Fuller, Elizabeth Peabody, and others of the transcendental group, were members of the Brook Farm community, or were warmly interested in its success. Margaret Fuller was a frequent visitor, and sometimes she remained there for weeks as a boarder. If she shared in Emerson's distrust of it as a practical experiment, and as a means of reforming society, she was drawn to its leading members by ties of closest friendship and appreciation. What has given Brook Farm an enduring interest and charm, so that its reputation grows with every year, is the fact that in one way or another all the transcendentalists were associated with it. It is a part of the literary history of the country, and gives it an element of romance. In no way is the literary quality of the association better shown than in the brilliant pages of "The Harbinger," — a journal that has never been surpassed in intellectual ability in this country.

While Brook Farm manifested one form of the transcendental movement, Thoreau in his hut on Walden pond, showed forth another. He was a representative of the extreme individualism of the time, but not its only exponent. A return to nature was desired by many men and women, even if they did not approve of solitary living in such manner as his. The gospel of manual labor was vigorously preached by them, and many attempts were made to give it concrete form. Several schools and colleges gave opportunity to their students to earn their way through them by physical toil; and farming, as well as several kinds of small manufacturing, were carried on in this way. More than one of the literary men of the time wished to take up farming, or some other form of practical industry, as a means of support while thus securing leisure for literary production. A motive to these efforts was a desire to know life as it is actually lived by the people. Thomas Wentworth Higginson has said of the period of his graduation at Harvard, in 1841 : " Without aid or guidance I was democratic in feeling, longed to know something of all sorts and conditions of men, and had a distinct feeling that I should like to be, for a year or two, a mechanic of some kind — a carpenter or blacksmith — in order to place myself in sympathy with all." Higginson carried this feeling so far as to make a vow of poverty, and to live in one of the cheapest college rooms while pursuing his post-graduate studies in Cambridge. In this way, he says, he enjoyed the same freedom that Thoreau secured in his hut. Another of his projects was to enter upon the cultivation of peaches, in order " to secure freedom for study and thought by moderate labor of the hands."

Lowell was infected by this ascetic spirit and this zeal for simplicity of life, and his biographer says " he allowed himself to dream of cultivating literature in solitude on a little oatmeal." He afterward wrote of himself, when a considerable sum of money had come to him from his wife's estate, after her death : " I confess I hardly feel so independent as before. I believe that in this age poverty needs to have apostles, and I had resolved to be one." Ellery Channing was of the same mind, apparently, and he spent several months in northern Illinois in splitting rails, living in a log hut erected by himself; and after he went to live in Concord he devoted a winter to wood-chopping in the woods of that town. A man as philosophic and moderate in temperament as George P. Bradford, after being for some months at Brook Farm, devoted himself to the growing of vegetables in Plymouth. In August, 1842, Hawthorne gave an account of a visit from him, and said in his journal: "He has been cultivating vegetables at Plymouth this summer, and selling them in the market. What a singular mode of life for a man of education and refinement, — to spend his days in hard and earnest bodily toil, and then to convey the products of his labor, in a wheelbarrow, to the public market, and there retail them out, — a peck of peas or beans, a bunch of turnips, a squash, a dozen ears of green corn! Few men, without some eccentricity of character, would have the moral strength to do this; and it is very striking to find such strength combined with utmost gentleness, and an uncommon regularity of nature. Occasionally he returns for a day or two to resume his place among scholars and idle people, as, for instance, the present week, when he has thrown aside his spade and hoe to attend the Commencement at Cambridge. He is a rare man, — a perfect original, yet without any one salient point; a character to be felt and understood, but almost impossible to describe."

In the spring of 1844 George William Curtis, accompanied by his brother Burrill, after having spent two years at Brook Farm as a student, went to Concord in order to acquire a practical acquaintance with country life and with agriculture. They devoted the forenoon of each day to laboring as farm-hands, while the afternoons and evenings were given to study and social recreation. The next summer they hired an acre or two of ground, cultivated it with their hands, and provided for their own wants, cooking their food and caring for their room.   They tramped to Wachusett and Monadnock, studied botany, read many books (George trying his hand at poetry), and gained health and strength.   At Plymouth, Marston Watson devoted himself to farming, and to the growing of apples, preferring these occupations to an academic or a professional career.   Mr. Sanborn calls Watson the Evelyn of New England, and says he "transformed a bare pasture-land into a beautiful park and garden, which became one of the favorite resorts of the Concord transcendentalists." The life of Thoreau on the shores of Walden pond is better understood in the light of these other experiments, and when it is remembered that one of his classmates at Harvard, Charles Stearns Wheeler, had tried the same kind of experiment as his a year or two before, and that Thoreau had spent several weeks with him in his shanty.   These ascetic revolts from the conventional ways of living had their motive in a desire for greater simplicity, for more of naturalness, and for the assertion of what is really essential.   They were attempts to realize plain living and high thinking in the actual conduct of life.

The transcendental movement is not fully understood until its humanitarian phases are carefully studied.   This element appears in Brook Farm, in the active labors of the transcendentalists in the cause of abolition, and in their efforts to promote reforms of many kinds.   If they were somewhat ascetic in their insistence upon a vegetarian diet, frequent ablutions, and a rigid plainness of living, they were eager to help their fellow-men in all practical ways.   In this direction no man had a greater influence than Dr. Channing, not so much because of his own labors as from the humanitarian incentives he gave to others.   Channing was all his life an invalid, compelled to nurse a feeble body, obliged to shut himself away from an active and aggressive life, compelled therefore to come little into actual contact with the rougher phases of human experience. He was by temperament a spiritual leader, and not a social reformer; and the motives that actuated him were religious and ideal. And yet, no man in this country has done so much as he to inspire other men with practical motives for the highest living and the noblest human service. Nurtured on his spiritual teaching, and inspired by his humanitarian spirit, he had amongst his disciples such persons as Emerson, Margaret Fuller, George Ripley, and a great number of others of like quality. He had also the gift to awaken the philanthropic labors of Samuel G. Howe, Dorothea Dix, Horace Mann, and Joseph Tuckerman, who were his friends, or listened from Sunday to Sunday to his preaching. When Tuckerman began to labor for the poor in Boston he had the encouragement and support of Channing. The splendid labors of Miss Dix for the insane were inspired by the spiritual teachings she received when she was a member of Channing's congregation in her youth. The heroic, if not romantic, labors of Dr. Howe for the Greeks, the blind, the idiotic, and all who were needy and distressed, had their motive in the teachings of Channing. It was when he listened to the great Federal Street preacher that Horace Mann became the leader of common-school education in America.

It was not Channing as a sectarian leader, as he is too often understood to have been, who aroused such men as have been named to engage in their humanitarian labors. He had no fondness for sect, no desire to create a new denomination. It was his high spiritual quality, his profoundly religious genius, akin in inward motive and outward expression to the best that there was in the transcendental movement, that gave him power to draw around him such a group of men and women. The tran-

scendentalists to a considerable degree followed his leadership, and were found foremost in reforms and every kind of
humanitarian effort. They were not mere closet philosophers or idle dreamers about what society ought to be; but
they worked wisely to educate the people, to save the unfortunate, and to bring the poor to ways of economy, self-
help, and good citizenship. It would not be just, however,
to claim that Mann and Tuckerman were in any distinct
sense transcendentalists or identified themselves with that
phase of thought; but the labors of these men marked the
time when this movement was in progress, and they shared
in the humanitarian tendencies that found expression in it.
And it is just to claim this because this movement had no
distinct limits, no set of phrases that defined it, nor any cult
to the promotion of which it was devoted. It was in reality
a movement, a spiritual temper, a practical attitude towards
life.

The men and women who are now named as giving character and purpose to the transcendental movement regarded
it as nothing more than a protest against conventionality,
and a desire for reality. It was to them a youthful spirit
of protest, an inclination to question and to criticise tradition, and an open-mindedness towards any suggestions that
would enable them to lead a natural life, and one that should
be earnestly ethical. The transcendentalists were not a sect
or a party in any sense; but they were a number of persons
more or less isolated from each other, who shared in the
faith that the spiritual life is a reality of ever-present power.
This power they trusted, and its law they obeyed. This
conviction that the spiritual life may appear in all forms
and take many names made it curiously varied in its manifestations. Emerson saw that it might appear in all churches,
and in the second volume of "The Dial" he set forth its
essential qualities with this vital statement: "We have
every day occasion to remark its [transcendentalism] per-

fect identity, under whatever new phraseology or application to new facts, with the liberal thought of all men of a religious and contemplative habit in other times and countries." It was characterized by its vitality, its earnestness, its sincerity. While it was critical, it was also constructive. It was not friendly to the forms of piety when they were forms only; and it was zealously devoted to what is inward and spiritual. Beginning as a spiritual protest, it ended as an effort to reconstruct society on the basis of ideal laws and practical duties. It was often visionary, it always sought reality; and it frequently inspired merchant and statesman, as well as artist and poet. Certain it is that it was the most vital influence that has ever come into American literature.

III

THE TRANSCENDENTAL CLUB

IN his "Historic Notes of Life and Letters in New England" Emerson mentions Edward Everett, Channing, Swedenborg, phrenology, the spirit of criticism, and other influences, as amongst those that were at work in the early part of the nineteenth century to produce "an eagerness for reform which showed itself in every quarter." One of these influences of first importance was the revival of the poetic spirit in England, especially by Coleridge and Wordsworth. Channing was largely indebted to Coleridge for incentives to his more spiritual interpretation of theological problems and for his idealism. When he was in England, in 1823, he visited Coleridge, and the latter wrote to Washington Allston of his American visitor: "He has the love of wisdom and the wisdom of love. I feel convinced," Coleridge also wrote, "that the few differences in opinion between Mr. Channing and myself not only are, but by him would be found to be, apparent, not real, — the same truth in different relations. Perhaps I have been more absorbed in the depth of the mystery of the spiritual life, he more engrossed by the loveliness of its manifestations." Elizabeth Peabody has enthusiastically recorded the interest Channing felt in the writings of Coleridge, and the satisfaction he found in his spiritual philosophy.

Channing was also largely indebted to Wordsworth for intellectual stimulus and satisfaction, and he had for him what his biographer called a "reverent affection." To Channing "The Excursion" came like a revelation. He read it constantly, and he admired it as one of the most

40

finished productions of the age. "Wordsworth's mingled reverence and freedom, loyalty and independence, manly simplicity and heroism, —his piety, trust, humility, profound conscience, and earnest aspiration, — his respectful, tender, appreciative love of man, recognizing greatness under lowliest disguises, and spreading sweet sanctions around every charity of social life, — his intense love of beauty, all-vivifying imagination, and mystical adorations of the Universe as the shadow of the Infinite Being, — his subjective habits of thought, metaphysically refined mode of observation, power of looking beneath all surfaces to the life, and beneath all forms to the spirit, — his high idealism, humanity, and hearty naturalness, in a word, combined to form a character with which Channing's was in full harmony."

This testimony of Channing's biographer to the influence upon him of Wordsworth would apply to nearly all the leaders of the transcendental movement. It was not so much the poetry of Wordsworth as his ideas, his interpretation of nature, and his spiritual conception of life, that awakened in them an enthusiastic response. It was in harmony with the individualism and the growing idealism that they knew at home, and they appreciated it all the more because it came from the leader of the new poetical school in England. It was not alone the new English poets, however, who were stirring fresh currents of life in the young men of America. "At this period of his life," says Channing's biographer, "he was breathing in the freshness with which the whole intellect of Christendom seemed inspired, as it pressed onward across the wide prairie which the science, philosophy, poetry, and revolutionary tendencies of the age had opened. It was with intense delight that he made acquaintance with the master minds of Germany, through the medium, first, of Madame de Staël, and afterward of Coleridge. He recognized in them his leaders. In Kant's doctrine of the Reason he found confirmation of the views which, in early years received from Price, had quickened him to ever deeper reverence for the essential powers of man. To Schelling's sublime intimations of the Divine Life everywhere manifested through nature and humanity, his heart, devoutly conscious of the universal agency of God, gladly responded. But above all did the heroic stoicism of Fichte charm him by its full assertion of the grandeur of the human will. Without adopting the systems of either of these philosophers, and, fortunately perhaps for him, without being fully acquainted with these systems, he yet received from their example the most animating incentives to follow out the paths of speculation into which his own had entered."

About the year 1815, graduates of Harvard College began to go to Europe for the completion of their studies. In that year Edward Everett went to Germany to prepare himself for the chair of Greek literature, and he remained until the autumn of 1819, over four years. He spent two years in Göttingen, and the rest of the time in travel and study, mostly in Germany. George Ticknor also went to Germany in 1815, and spent two years at Göttingen. In 1817, George Bancroft followed, staying two years at Göttingen, and a like period at Berlin, where he knew Schleiermacher, von Humboldt, Varnhagen von Ense, and other notable men. Frederic H. Hedge went to Germany under the charge of Bancroft, at the age of twelve, remained there five years as a student, and returned in 1823.

These men, on their return, largely increased the interest in German literature and philosophy. Emerson has given a glowing account of the influence of Edward Everett. "Germany had created criticism in vain for us, until 1820," Emerson says, "when Edward Everett returned from his five years in Europe, and brought to Cambridge his rich results, which no one was so fitted by natural grace and the splendor of his rhetoric to introduce and recommend. The novelty of the learning lost nothing in the skill and genius of his relation, and the rudest undergraduate found a new morning opened to him in the lecture-room of Harvard Hall. There was an influence on the young people from the genius of Everett which was almost comparable to that of Pericles in Athens. . . . The word that he spoke, and the manner in which he spoke it, became current and classical in New England. . . . By a series of lectures, largely and fashionably attended for two winters in Boston, he made a beginning of popular and miscellaneous lecturing, which in that region at least had important results. I am quite certain that this purely literary influence was of the first importance to the American mind."

What Everett did was to prepare for the acceptance of German ways of thinking on the part of young men, — not that he was himself in any strict sense a transcendentalist. Bancroft did become an idealist as the result of his German studies, and Hedge was one of the leaders of the transcendental movement. The latter was the only one, however, taking a prominent part in that movement, who studied in Germany or came into immediate contact with its philosophical leaders. The others were indebted to the influence of Coleridge, and more especially to that of Carlyle. William Emerson went to Göttingen in 1823, and as a result he was not able to become a minister. His brother Waldo was at this time little interested in German thought, and did not give his attention to it until Carlyle had turned his interest in that direction. In 1829 he was reading Coleridge and Swedenborg, with the result that he came more and more to detach religion from all forms. Soon after he was reading Carlyle's articles in the English Reviews, and in 1833 he visited that brilliant writer in his home at Craigenputtoch. At the same time he sought out and made the acquaintance of Coleridge, Wordsworth, and Landor. On his return from this European visit Emerson had his little book on Nature already in preparation. It will be seen, therefore, that Emerson was only in a small degree indebted to the German thinkers for his philosophy. So late as 1836, when the transcendental club came into existence, Hedge was the only one of those connected with it, according to his own statement, " who had any first-hand acquaintance with the German transcendental philosophy." During the month of June, 1835, Emerson set down in his journal what he had come to regard as the primary laws of the mind, part of his statement being as follows:

"These laws are ideas of Reason; they astonish the Understanding, and seem to it gleams of a world in which we do not live. Our compound nature differences us from God, but our reason is not to be distinguished from the Divine Essence. To call it ours seems an impertinence, so absolute and unconfined is it. The best we can say of God we mean of the mind as it is known to us. Time and space are below its sphere; it considers things according to more intimate properties; it beholds their essence, wherein is seen what they can produce. It is in all men, even the worst, and constitutes them men."

Although George Ripley did not study in Germany, he was one of the first to make known in a scholarly form the work of the great German thinkers. He also gave much attention to the French idealists or eclectics, as they have been called. So early as 1830 he was writing in "The Christian Examiner," the September number of that year containing a paper by him on Degerando's theory of self-education as self-development. He followed with papers on Pestalozzi, Herder, Schleiermacher, as well as upon Mackintosh and Martineau. In 1836 he published six "Discourses on the Philosophy of Religion Addressed to Doubters who wish to Believe," in which he set forth the new spiritual philosophy with calm reasoning and true insight. But his most important work in making known the French and German thinkers was in editing the fourteen volumes of the "Specimens of Foreign Standard Literature," which were published in Boston by Hilliard, Gray and Co., from 1838 to 1842. The first two volumes of "Philosophical Miscellanies" were translated by Ripley himself from Cousin, Jouffroy, and Benjamin Constant, with a lengthy introduction reviewing and condemning the influence of sensationalism, followed by extended notes in interpretation of the authors presented. The third volume contained John S. Dwight's translations from Goethe, Schiller, and other German poets; and the fourth, Margaret Fuller's translation of Eckermann's "Conversations with Goethe." In two volumes W. H. Channing gave Jouffroy's "Introduction to Ethics" to the American public; and in three volumes C. C. Felton added Menzel's "History of German Literature." Then followed in two volumes De Wette's "Theodore, or the Skeptic's Conversion," by J. F. Clarke; and the same author's "Human Life, or Practical Ethics," in two volumes, was added by Samuel Osgood. The series concluded with "Songs and Ballads from the German," by C. T. Brooks. While these volumes did not all move in the direction of transcendentalism, they were in aid of the movement towards a broader interpretation of life and literature. Although these books were long since out of print, and though few of them passed into a second edition, they served an important purpose in making known some of the leading authors and thinkers of Europe.

Another leader in making known the works of the German thinkers was Frederic Henry Hedge. In March, 1833, he published in "The Christian Examiner" an article based on the republication of the chief works of Coleridge by President James Marsh, of the University of Vermont, in 1829 and 1831. After reviewing the philosophical work of Coleridge, Hedge passed on to discuss the "transcendental philosophers" of Germany, defending them and giving an accurate statement of their point of view. He says: "There is only one point from which we can clearly understand and decide upon the speculations of Kant and his followers; that point is the interior consciousness distinguished from the common consciousness by its being an active and not a passive state. In the language of the school it is a free intuition, and can only be attained by a vigorous effort of the will. . . . The pre-eminence of Germany among the nations in our day in respect of intellectual culture is universally acknowledged; and we do fully believe that whatever excellence that nation has attained in science, in history, or poetry, is mainly owing to the influence of her philosophy, to the faculty which that philosophy has imparted of seizing on the spirit of every question, and determining at once the point of view from which each subject should be regarded, — in one word, the transcendental method. . . . A philosophy which has given such an impulse to mental culture and scientific research, which has done so much to establish and to extend the spiritual in man, needs no apology; it commends itself by its fruits, and must ever live, though the name of its founder be forgotten, and not one of its doctrines survive."

In 1848 Hedge published "The Prose Writers of Germany," a work of importance in making known in this country the leading German authors. Several other volumes published by him led to the same result, that of giving a wider currency to the conclusions of the idealistic philosophy, especially as they bear upon theological problems. He was not alone, however, in applying transcendentalism to theology, for so early as 1834 James Walker, afterwards president of Harvard College, preached a sermon that was printed in two or three different forms, in which he maintained "that a foundation for religion is laid in the soul of man, the existence whereof is attested and put beyond controversy by the revelations of consciousness." His subject

was " The Philosophy of Man's Spiritual Nature in Regard
to the Foundations of Faith," and his purpose was to prove
that " religion in the soul, consisting as it does of a manifestation and development of man's spiritual faculties and
capacities, is a reality in itself." In 1836 Convers Francis,
for twenty years a professor in the Harvard Divinity
School, published an essay on " Christianity as a Purely
Internal System," in which he said that Christianity " is
a purely internal religion," and that it "was the first
and only system which professed to build its kingdom
within the soul of man." " There is great sublimity," he
said, " in this internal, quiet, spirit-searching character of
Christianity."

All these men were transcendentalists, though it may be
in a vague and indefinite manner. They were not organized
into a school, and they had no well-rounded system to prescribe and defend. To a large extent, as yet, they were
solitary students, who were dissatisfied with the older
materialistic and sensuous systems ; but they were not
agreed as to what should be put in place of them. Perhaps
they were agreed only in being dissatisfied with the old,
and in aspiring to something nobler and more spiritual
in its purpose. Probably no one had used the word
"transcendental" earlier than Hedge, as already quoted,
and with him it meant the activity of the interior consciousness, or spiritual intuition. To Emerson it meant, as he
said in his little book on Nature, that "man is conscious
of a universal soul within or behind his individual life."
These ideas had not yet been clarified ; but they were
enough to bring together those who held them for purposes
of consultation and encouragement. The first meeting of
this kind seems to have been held in the autumn of 1836,
in connection with the bicentennial celebration of the found-
ing of Harvard College. At that time four young Unitarian ministers — R. W. Emerson, F. H. Hedge, George

Ripley, and George Putnam — came together for conversation after the conclusion of the exercises of the day, and began to discuss the narrow tendencies of thought in the churches. Adjourning to Willard's Hotel they continued their conversation, with the result that they agreed the subject was worthy of more serious consideration. Accordingly, they met at the house of George Ripley, Chauncy Street, Boston, September 19, 1836; and there were present Ripley, Emerson, Hedge, Alcott, Clarke, and Francis, and one or two divinity students.

In his account of the origin of this club Emerson attributes it to the influence of Dr. Channing, and indicates that it was but a casual gathering of friends, without definite organization or purpose. "Dr. Channing took counsel in 1840 with George Ripley, to the point whether it were possible to bring cultivated, thoughtful people together, and make society that deserved the name." This evidently is in reference to those meetings that culminated in the organization of Brook Farm; but what Emerson says in the next paragraph indicates that he attributed the origin of the transcendental club to the same date, which is a mistake. Still confusing Brook Farm and the transcendental club, he describes how the latter had its origin. "Some time afterwards," he says, "Dr. Channing opened his mind to Mr. and Mrs. Ripley, and with some care they invited a limited party of ladies and gentlemen [Brook Farm]. I had the honor to be present. Though I recall the fact, I do not retain any instant consequence of this attempt, or any connection between it and the new zeal of the friends who at that time [transcendental club, four years earlier] began to be drawn together by sympathy of studies and of aspiration. Margaret Fuller, George Ripley, Dr. Convers Francis, Theodore Parker, Dr. Hedge, Mr. Brownson, James Freeman Clarke, William H. Channing, and many others, gradually drew together, and from time to time spent an afternoon at each other's houses in a serious conversation."

In his biography of Alcott, Mr. F. B. Sanborn indicates that the second meeting of the club (the first being at Ripley's) was held at the house of Mr. Alcott (26 Beach Street, Boston) in October, 1836. He says there were present Emerson, George Ripley, F. H. Hedge, Orestes A. Brownson, J. F. Clarke, and C. A. Bartol, besides the host. The subject discussed was "American Genius, — the causes which hinder its growth." Colonel Higginson appears to indicate that the second meeting was held in Concord with Emerson, but this was probably the third meeting, and he overlooks that held with Alcott. At the Concord meeting there were present Brownson, Bartol, Parker, Stetson, and others, who were not at the house of Ripley at the first meeting; and there were also present Margaret Fuller and Elizabeth P. Peabody,

The account given of the origin of the club by Dr. Hedge is of interest, as it differs in some details from those of others. He says that in Cambridge he chanced to confer together with Emerson and Ripley "on the state of current opinion in theology and philosophy, which we agreed," he says, "in thinking very unsatisfactory. Could anything be done in the way of protest and introduction of deeper and broader views ? What precisely we wanted, it would have been difficult for either of us to state. What we strongly felt was dissatisfaction with the reigning sensuous philosophy, dating from Locke, on which our Unitarian theology was based. The writings of Coleridge, recently edited by Marsh, and some of Carlyle's earlier essays, especially the ' Characteristics ' and the 'Signs of the Times,' had created a ferment in the minds of some of the young clergy of that day. There was a promise in the air of a new era of intellectual life. We four concluded to call a few like-minded seekers together on the following week.

Some dozen of us met in Boston, at the house, I believe, of Mr. Ripley. Among them I recall the names of Orestes Brownson [probably not present at this first meeting, however], Cyrus Bartol [also evidently not present at the first meeting], Theodore Parker [not at Ripley's], and Wheeler and Bartlett, tutors in Harvard College. There was some discussion, but no conclusion reached, on the question whether it were best to start a new journal as the organ of our views, or to work through those already existing. The next meeting, in the same month (October), was held by invitation of Emerson, at his house in Concord. A large number assembled; besides some of those who met in Boston, I remember Mr. Alcott, John S. Dwight, Ephraim Peabody, Dr. Convers Francis, Mrs. Sarah Ripley, Miss Elizabeth Peabody, Margaret Fuller, Caleb Stetson, James Freeman Clarke. These were the earliest of a series of meetings held from time to time, as occasion prompted, for seven or eight years. Jones Very was one of those who occasionally attended; H. D. Thoreau another. There was no club, properly speaking; no organization, no presiding officer, no vote ever taken. How the name transcendental, given to these gatherings and the set of persons who took part in them, originated, I cannot say. It certainly never was assumed by the persons so called."

One of the most interesting accounts of the origin of the club was that given by Alcott, in one of his conversations. Of the first meeting, at the house of George Ripley, he said: "It was a preliminary meeting, to see how far it would be possible for earnest minds to meet, and with the least possible formality communicate their views. They dispensed with any election of a chairman; if there was to be any precedency, it naturally belonged to the oldest. At that time the oldest of that company was Mr. Francis. They gave invitations to Dr. Channing, Jonathan Phillips, Rev. James Walker, Rev. N. L. Frothingham, Rev. J. S. Dwight,

Rev. W. H. Channing, and Rev. C. A. Bartol, to join with them if they chose to do so. The three last named appeared afterwards and met the club frequently. They adjourned to meet at Mr. Alcott's house in Beac... Street, on the afternoon of October 3, 1836, at three o'clock. On that occasion," Mr. Alcott continued, " the subject of discussion was this: American Genius, — the causes which hinder its growth giving us no first-rate productions. There were present at that second meeting, Emerson, Hedge, Francis, Ripley, Brownson, Clarke, Bartol, and the host. Subsequent meetings took place in Boston the following winter and spring, and at Concord and Watertown, then the home of Mr. Francis, during the summer of 1837. So far as there was any show of order in these meetings, it was somewhat like this: the senior member, Mr. Francis, — the company being seated, — would invite the members, as they sat, to make remarks, which they did. I believe there was seldom an inclination on the part of any one to be silent. Always, or nearly always, every person present contributed something to the conversation. At that time theology was the theme of general discussion. Dr. Beecher had come to Boston a few years before to put down Unitarianism, as he fondly fancied, by preaching his Puritan views, — the views of Calvin. These, however, had passed away, in good measure ; and the views of Professor Norton of the Divinity School were then in the ascendant. Dr. Channing had published his essays in 'The Christian Examiner;' he was also preaching when he was able.

"There were added to the club, or symposium, in 1837, Stetson, Parker, Margaret Fuller, and Elizabeth Peabody. Rev. Thomas T. Stone afterwards joined it. At the meetings of the club, Mr. Emerson was almost always present. On not more than two or three occasions during the three or four years that the club met — four or five times a year, probably — was he absent. Indeed, the members looked

forward with great delight to the opportunity of meeting
him. They were presently scattered abroad; but it was
arranged that during the season of recreation, when these
persons came to the city, the meetings should be held quite
often. They were held at Watertown, Newton, Concord,
Milton, Chelsea (where Brownson was then living), frequently in Boston, and perhaps elsewhere. I remember the
doctrine of Personality came up for discussion. It was the
fashion to speak against personality, — the orthodox view
of it ; and the favorite phrase was impersonality. In at-
tempting to liberate the true view from the superstitions
which had gathered about it in coming down through Cal-
vinism, through Puritanism, some made the mistake of conceiving individuality to be the central thought ; and at
these meetings that subject was discussed. To show how
the topics about which I have been speaking interested the
club, in May, 1838, the same company again met, — Rev.
N. L. Frothingham being present for the first time, and the
only time that I ever saw him, — at Medford ; and we discussed this question : 'Is Mysticism an Element of Christianity?' That question touched the seat and root of things.
Jones Very's poems and essays were published in September, 1839. Very significant they were, too; as if, in
answer to the inquiry whether mysticism was an element in
Christianity, here was an illustration of it in a living person,
himself present at the club. They are very remarkable
poems and essays. There had been nothing printed until
Emerson's 'Nature,' unless it may have been Sampson
Reed's little book called 'The Growth of the Mind,' which
had intimated genius of the like subtle, chaste, and simple
quality."

By the members this club was often spoken of amongst
themselves as "Hedge's Club," because it was held when
Frederic H. Hedge, who became the minister of the Unitarian church in Bangor, Maine, in 1835, was able to be

in Boston. In his diary Alcott calls it "The Symposium Club." Alcott put down the names of sixteen persons in his diary as constituting the regular members of the club. These were Convers Francis, Emerson, Alcott, Ripley, Hedge, Clarke, Bartol, Margaret Fuller, Elizabeth P. Peabody, Parker, W. H. Channing, Dwight, Jones Very, Thoreau, Robert Bartlett, and Caleb Stetson. The occasional attendants included Dr. Channing, Brownson, Charles Follen, Samuel J. May, William Russell, George Bancroft, Christopher Cranch, S. G. Ward, Mrs. Samuel (Sarah) Ripley, Miss Elizabeth Hoar, Thomas T. Stone, George P. Bradford, Le Baron Russell, and William D. Wilson. Probably several of these names should be added to the sixteen mentioned by Alcott as those of regular members.

Among the subjects discussed by the club were Law, Truth, Individuality, Theology, Revelation, Inspiration, Providence, the Personality of God. At one meeting Ripley took exceptions to the impersonal conception of God presented by Emerson in a remarkable lecture he had just delivered in one of his courses of lectures. At another meeting the subject was the Progress of Civilization, and Parker recorded in his diary that Dr. Channing and Ripley discussed it " with great power of thought and richness of eloquence." " Had the conversation of this evening," he there wrote, " been written out by Plato, it would equal any of his beautiful dialogues." The club was continued until about 1850, meeting once a month, though without much regularity, and usually with Emerson in Concord, Francis in Watertown, or Bartol in Boston.

The occasional and friendly character of the club has been well described by Emerson, though with perhaps too much depreciation of its actual value to those who took part in its meetings. " These fine conversations," he says, " were incomprehensible to some in the company, and they had their revenge in their little joke. One declared that 'it seemed to him like going to heaven in a swing;' another reported that, at a knotty point in the discourse, a sympathizing Englishman with a squeaking voice interrupted with the question, 'Mr. Alcott, a lady near me desires to inquire whether omnipotence abnegates attribute.'"

"I think there prevailed at that time a general belief in Boston that there was some concert of doctrinaires to establish certain opinions and inaugurate some movement in literature, philosophy, and religion, of which design the supposed conspirators were quite innocent; for there was no concert, and only here and there two or three men or women who read and wrote, each alone, with unusual vivacity. Perhaps they only agreed in having fallen upon Coleridge and Wordsworth and Goethe, then on Carlyle, with pleasure and sympathy. Otherwise their education and reading were not marked, but had the American superficialness, and their studies were solitary. I suppose all of them were surprised at this rumor of a school or sect, and certainly at the name of Transcendentalism, given nobody knows by whom, or when it was applied. As these persons became in the common chances of society acquainted with each other, there resulted certainly strong friendships, which of course were exclusive in proportion to their heat; and perhaps those persons who were mutually the best friends were the most private and had no ambition of publishing their letters, diaries, or conversation.

"From that time meetings were held for conversation, with very little form, from house to house, of people engaged in studies, fond of books, and watchful of all the intellectual light from whatever quarter it flowed. Nothing could be less formal, yet the intelligence and character and varied ability of the company gave it some notoriety, and perhaps waked curiosity as to its aims and results."

The service of the club was that of bringing together "the like-minded," and of making them acquainted with each.

The friendships that resulted were of much importance to these pioneers in a great intellectual movement. Such men as Emerson, Parker, and Alcott, would doubtless have made their way alone to such conclusions as they ultimately reached; but to most of the others there was need of encouragement and support in the search for a larger statement of truth than had been hitherto customary. Even the leaders found help in the support of those they respected and admired. On the whole, therefore, the club was a necessary help to all concerned, even though none of them expressed a large debt to it for mental stimulus and spiritual quickening.

The club was for a dozen years the visible expression of one of the most important mental movements this country has known. Its chief value was in its effects upon our literature. There was too much in the club of enthusiasm, too much of romantic anticipation, too much of froth and folly; but there was also much of bold initiative, daring innovation, and courage to look at life as it is. The result was that the old ways were forsaken, and fresh life and truthfulness came into our literature. It cannot be said that the club was in itself the cause of this literary revival, but it was one of its most interesting expressions. The same tendencies that brought together these young men and women were putting new life into the nation, new faith into religion, new purpose into ethics. When it is considered what these men and women accomplished, how great an addition they have made to our intellectual history, it will be recognized that this little club, informal as it was, produced great and important results.

IV

THE ORIGIN OF THE DIAL

THE chief importance of the transcendental club was that in it was originated "The Dial," the first really independent and original journal published in this country. Excellent monthlies and quarterlies had been published previously, but they were imitative of European ideas and methods, and they had no fresh literary merit. In a large degree such periodicals as "The North American Review" and "The Christian Examiner," both of them then published in Boston, were academic in taste, pedantic in method, and wanting in literary insight. "The Dial" did not wholly escape these limitations, but it took a new course, and one that was not only original, but initiative of better things in the future. It was its novelty, its freshness of tone, its romantic temper, its boundless hope and courage, that caused it to be criticised and jeered at generally by the more conservative literary journals. It was not conformatory enough to the old methods to secure it a general recognition on the part of the public; and it was condemned because it was not understood or appreciated.

So early as 1834 or 1835 there was discussed the starting of a journal to represent the new way of thinking, even previous to the organization of the transcendental club, in 1836. Early in 1835 it was the subject of frequent consultations, but the first published mention of it appears in a letter from Emerson to Carlyle, dated March 12, 1835. In speaking of the influence of Dr. Channing, Emerson says: "He [Channing] lay awake all night, he told my friend last week, because he had learned in the evening that some young men proposed to issue a journal, to be called 'The Transcendentalist,' as the organ of a spiritual philosophy. . . I intimated above that we aspire to have a work on the First Philosophy in Boston. I hope, or wish rather. Those that are forward in it debate upon the name. I doubt not in the least its reception if the material that should fill it existed. Through the thickest understanding will the reason throw itself instantly into relation with the truth that is its object, whenever that appears."

In his next letter to Carlyle, written from Concord, April 30, 1835, Emerson pleads with his friend to come to America, and sets forth in strongest terms the reasons for so doing. After describing his friend's popularity, the cost of living, and the support he could be sure of obtaining by lecturing and authorship, he enumerates what was said on the other side by the doubters, and adds : " However, it was suggested that if Mr. C., would undertake a Journal, of which we have talked much, but which we have never yet produced, he would do us great service, and we feel some confidence that it could be made to secure him a support. It is that project which I mentioned to you in a letter by Mr. Barnard [the one of March 12], — a book to be called ' The Transcendentalist,' or 'The Spiritual Inquirer,' or the like, and of which F. H. Hedge was to be the editor. Those who are most interested in it designed to make gratuitous contributions to its pages, until its success could be assured. Hedge is just leaving our neighborhood to be settled as a minister two hundred and fifty miles off, in Maine, and entreats that you will edit the journal. He will write, and I please myself with thinking I shall be able to write under such auspices."

Carlyle did not find it in his way to come to America, though Emerson wrote : " We feel some confidence that it could be made to secure him a support." The writing of " The French Revolution," ill-health, and other causes, probably

more important than all, his reluctance to change his place
of habitation, made this project, however strongly urged by
Emerson and others, quite unavailing. As a result, there
being no one else to edit the proposed journal, it was not
undertaken. It was the interest in it, however, that led to
the formation of the transcendental club. The journal itself
seems to have received little attention until 1839, when it
was again a frequent subject for discussion. The cause of
the revival of interest in the publication of a journal was
that "The Monthly Magazine," started in London by John
A. Heraud, with January, 1839, in some degree answered
to what had been projected in Boston. It was read with
delight by Alcott, Francis, Ripley, and others; and its contents were discussed and warmly approved. Its character
was much more distinctly literary than "The Dial" became,
but it had much of the idealistic spirit of the time, and it
was saturated with the philosophic thought imbibed from
Coleridge and from Germany. The writings of Emerson and
Alcott were hailed with delight in its pages, "Nature" being
attributed to the latter. In April, 1840, it published a
master's oration, by Robert Bartlett, a recent graduate at
Harvard, which contained the essence of the thought that
was stirring many minds in America. It was proposed on
the part of this magazine to publish articles and poems by
the Boston writers, including Margaret Fuller, Dwight, and
others; but nothing came of this proposition. Other English journals of a like nature, though more ethereal and indefinite, were begun, and lived their little day. Alcott read
all of these, and with much regret that something as good
could not be produced on this side the Atlantic. Writing
in his diary, under date of November, 1839, he said: "It
will be some time before our contemplated journal will be
commenced, and I question whether we shall find talent or
spirit to equal that of our English brethren. We have
writers enough, but they are neither accomplished nor free.

Half a dozen men exhaust our list of contributors; Emerson, Hedge, Miss Fuller, Ripley, Channing, Dwight, and Clarke, are our dependence."

In his diary for September 28, 1839, Alcott again made record of his ideas in regard to the publication of a transcendental journal. " I had an agreeable talk with G. Ripley on the times," he wrote, " and particularly on my transatlantic friends. He is much taken with Heraud's journal, which he has read from January last. He wishes to establish a journal of like character among ourselves. We need such an organ, but lack the ability to make it worthy of our position. There are but few contributors, and those not at all free from the influence of the past. Yet such a journal we must have in due time. Doubtless it would succeed even now. Brownson's ' Boston Quarterly,' is pledged to a party in Politics [Democrat], and takes narrow ground in philosophy and literature. We must have a free journal for the soul which awaits its scribes."

In the meantime an effort had actually been made to secure the publication of the projected journal. At a meeting of the Symposium, as the transcendental club was often called, held at the house of Cyrus A. Bartol, September 18, 1839, Margaret Fuller was present, and gave her views in regard to what it should be and how it should be conducted. There were also present Parker, Hedge, Ripley, Alcott, W. H. Channing, and the host. Alcott spoke of his diary, to which he had given the title of " The Dial," and proposed that this should be the name of the new periodical. After this meeting Brownson attempted to secure the support of the projectors of " The Dial " to his " Boston Quarterly Review," which he had established in 1838, as an independent journal of liberal thought. It was his desire that the transcendentalists should write in his review instead of starting one of their own. Alcott consulted with Emerson and Margaret Fuller in regard to this proposition ; but it was not acceptable to them, — Brownson's dogmatism, and his political relations standing in the way of such an alliance. Moreover, the transcendentalists were of a mind to have a journal wholly their own, that should speak their word with no indistinctness of utterance.

A name having been agreed upon for the new journal, and Margaret Fuller having been selected as the editor, she began the search for contributors ,with the purpose of issuing the first number in April, 1840. She wrote to William Henry Channing, then preaching in Cincinnati, January 1, 1840, to secure his aid : " I write to inform you that there is now every reason to hope that a first number of the much talked of new journal may be issued next April, and to ask what you will give. I have counted on you for the first number, because you seemed so really in earnest and said you had articles ready written. But I want to know what part you propose to take in the grand symphony, and I pray you to answer me directly, for we must proceed to tune the instruments. Mr. Emerson is warmly interested, and will give active assistance for a year. Mr. Ripley and Mr. Dwight are also in earnest ; for others I know not yet. Will not Mr. Vaughan give us some aid ? His article on the Chartists excited interest here, and we should like some such ' large sharp strokes ' of the pen very much. . . At Newport you prophesied a new literature ; shall it dawn in 1840 ? "

In reply to this urgent request for aid to the proposed journal, Channing wrote, on February 25 : " You ask me what part I proposed to play in the grand concert. Frankly, I intended to be a listener only ; but I am not so selfish and lazy as to grudge any aid which my efforts can give. I fear much that we shall be obliged to give up our publication here [' The Western Messenger '] ; and in that case I should with a better prospect unite with you, for I could better command my time and thought. Do tell me, when you write, more of your plans, and of the proposed character of this periodical; I can then judge better whether I am competent to lend any efficient assistance. I have heard from my sister delightful accounts of your success [in her conversations], and break the tenth commandment often in coveting my neighbor's goods. For myself, I find my chief pleasure in opening to my hearers my whole soul. Week by week I give them the best which the time sends of truth and life,— and I trust some seeds of future peace are sown. But I confess to you I am restless, and not energetic enough to make for myself the sphere I crave. I walk in a consciousness of unemployed force, and see not the when nor the how to make a world out of my chaos. My social nature is defective; joyfully would I take a few lessons from you in the art of aiding others to find their own souls. This, however, cannot be very edifying or interesting to you, so I will close up the log-book of my voyage."

Writing the same day, January 1, to Hedge, she said the same word, but in a somewhat different tone. "I write this New Year's Day to wish you all happiness," she begins, "and to say that there is reason to expect the new journal (in such dim prospect when you were here) may see the light next April. And we depend on you for the first number, and for solid bullion too. Mr. Emerson will write, every number, and so will you if you are good and politic, for it is the best way to be heard from your sentry-box there in Bangor. My friend, I really hope you will make this the occasion for assailing the public ear with such a succession of melodies that all the stones will advance to form a city of refuge for the just. I think with the greatest pleasure of working in company with you. But what will it be ? will you give us poems or philosophy or criticism, and how much ? for we are planning out our first number by the yard. Let me hear from you directly."

The first number of "The Dial" had nothing from the pen of Hedge, perhaps not because these pleadings of the editor were unavailing, for each of the following two numbers contained productions of his, an essay and a poem. Evidently he had too many other tasks in hand to yield at once to her demands, for on March 10 she wrote him again. "Henry, I adjure you," she pleads, " in the name of the Genii, Muses, Pegasus, Apollo, Pollio, Apollyon (and must I mention . . .), to send me something good for this journal before the 1st May. All mortals, my friend, are slack and bare ; they wait to see whether Hotspur wins, before they levy aid for as good a plan as ever was laid. I know you are plagued and it is hard to write ; just so is it with me, for I also am a father. But you can help, and become a godfather ! if you like, and let it be nobly, for if the first number justify not the magazine, it will not find justification ; so write, my friend, write ; and paint not for me fine plans on the clouds to be achieved at some future time, as others do who have had many years to be thinking of immortality.

"I could make a number myself with the help Mr. Emerson will give, but the Public, I trow, is too astute a donkey not to look sad at that." The reference here is to the lines in the "Rejected Addresses" :

> "And when that donkey looked me in the face
> Its face was sad ; and you are sad, my Public ! "

As we follow the correspondence of Margaret Fuller we are able to trace the growth in her mind of her idea of a truly representative journal, though it never came to be clear and positive. To her the purpose had in view was somewhat indistinct, not because she was incapable of formulating a plan for the proposed journal, but because her aims were too high and impracticable. Her plans were too ideal, too little controlled by anything in the way of experience, and too far away from what would appeal to the public, even that with which she was connected. Her chief desire was for a perfectly free journal, that should be suggestive rather than dogmatic, and capable of awakening the best that was in each of its readers. This purpose she set forth in a letter written March 22, 1840. " I have a great deal written," she says to this friend, " but as I read it over, scarce a word seems pertinent to the place or time. . . . What others can do, — whether all that has been said is the mere restlessness of discontent, or there are thoughts really struggling for utterance, — will be tested now. A perfectly free organ is to be offered for the expression of individual thought and character. There are no party measures to be carried, no particular standard to be set up. A fair, calm tone, a recognition of universal principles, will, I hope, pervade the essays in every form. I trust there will be a spirit neither of dogmatism nor of compromise, and that this journal will aim, not at leading public opinion, but at stimulating each man to judge for himself, and to think more deeply and more nobly, by letting him see how some minds are kept alive by a wise self-trust. We must not be sanguine as to the amount of talent which will be brought to bear on this publication. All concerned are rather indifferent, and there is no great promise for the present. We cannot show high culture, and I doubt about vigorous thought. But we shall manifest free action as far as it goes, and a high aim. It were much if a periodical could be kept open, not to accomplish any outward object, but merely to afford an avenue for what of liberal and calm thought might be originated among us, by the wants of individual minds."

From this letter it will be seen that Margaret Fuller's distrust of herself and of her contributors was very great, that her ideal was quite above what she felt could be attained. She expected to fill the pages of her journal without paying for the contributions, and that made it impossible she should secure the best work of a corps of regular writers. However willing her friends might be to aid, however desirous of the success of "The Dial," it was practically impossible to secure their stated help in that way.

A letter written April 19 indicates very clearly that she regarded " The Dial" as an experiment, and with much of doubt as to the outcome. "Things go on pretty well," she writes, " but doubtless people will be disappointed, for they seem to be looking for the Gospel of Transcendentalism. . . . Mr. Emerson knows best what he wants; but he has already said it in various ways. Yet this experiment is well worth trying; hearts beat so high, they must be full of something, and here is a way to breathe it out quite freely. It is for dear New England that I want this review. For myself, if I had wished to write a few pages now and then, there were ways and means enough of disposing of them. But in truth I have not much to say; for since I have had leisure to look at myself, I find that, so far from being an original genius, I have not yet learned to think to any depth, and that the utmost I have done in life has been to form my character to a certain consistency, cultivate my tastes, and learn to tell the truth with a little better grace than I did at first. For this the world will not care much, so I shall hazard a few critical remarks only, or an unpretending chalk-sketch now and then, till I have learned to do something. There will be beautiful poesies; about prose we know not yet so well. We shall be the means of publishing the little Charles Emerson left as a mark of his noble course, and though it lies in fragments, all who read it will be gainers." In the same letter, probably addressed to W. H. Channing, she speaks of the part in the enterprise she proposed to take herself. " I do not expect to be of much use except to urge on the laggards and scold the lukewarm," is her modest statement, " and act like Helen McGregor to those who love compromise, by doing my little best to sink them in the waters of oblivion."

Emerson wrote somewhat more hopefully of the new venture, perhaps because he had not upon him the burden of its editing. He was wholly disinclined to that task, as he said in a letter to his brother William in New York, under date of September 26, 1839. " George Ripley and others revive at this time the old project of a new journal for the exposition of absolute truth," he wrote; " but I doubt a little if it reach the day. I will never be editor, though I am counted on as a contributor. My Henry Thoreau will be a great poet for such a company ; and one of these days for all companies." On December 12 he wrote to Margaret Fuller in much the same mood. " I believe we all feel much alike in regard to this journal," he says to her. " We all wish it to be, but do not wish to be in any way personally responsible for it. For the sake of the brilliant possibility I would promise honest labor of some sort to each number for a year, but I should wish to leave myself the latitude of supreme indifference, nay abhorrence of such modes of working forever after. But if your labors shall introduce a new age, they will also mould our opinions, and we shall think what you think."

In a letter to Carlyle, dated March 18, he also refers to "The Dial." "Did I tell you," he asks, " that we hope shortly to send you some American verses and prose of good intent ? My vivacious friend Margaret Fuller is to edit a journal whose first number she promises for the 1st of July next, which I think will be written with a good will if written at all. I saw some poetical fragments which charmed me, — if only the writer consents to give them to the public." "I have very good hope," he writes April 21, "that my friend Margaret Fuller's Journal — after many false baptisms, now saying it will be called ' The Dial,' and which is to appear in July — will give you a better knowledge of our young people than any you have had. I will see that it goes to you when the sun first shines on its face. I have contrived to read almost every volume of Goethe, and I have fifty-five, but I have read nothing else; but I have not now looked even into Goethe for a long time. There is no great need that I should discourse to you on books, least of all on his books; but in a lecture on Literature, in my course last winter, I blurted all my nonsense on that subject, and who knows but Margaret Fuller may be glad to print it and send it to you? I know not."

In his next letter to Carlyle, June 30, Emerson mentions his lecture on Literature as having been sent to Margaret Fuller for "The Dial," but that it had been crowded out and would not appear until October. "With this, or presently after it," he writes, "I shall send a copy of 'The Dial.' It is not yet much; indeed, though no copy has come to me, I know it is far short of what it should be, for they have suffered puffs and dulness to creep in for the sake of the complement of pages; but it is better than anything we had; and I have some poetry communicated to me for the next number which I wish Sterling and Milnes to see. In this number what say you to the Elegy ['Sympathy'] written by a youth who grew up in this town and lives near me, — Henry Thoreau? A criticism on 'Persius' is his also. From the papers of my brother Charles, I gave them the fragments on Homer, Shakespeare, Burke; and my brother Edward wrote the little 'Farewell,' when last he left his home. The 'Address of the Editors to the Readers' is all the prose that is mine, and whether they have printed a few verses for me I do not know."

What Emerson said to Carlyle of the pages of the new journal being filled by young people may in a degree account for its failure to give him that which he desired. When the first number of "The Dial" appeared, its chief contributors were still young, some of them even youthful.

Ripley was thirty-eight; Emerson, thirty-seven ; and Hedge, thirty-five. Margaret Fuller, Parker, W. H. Channing, and Clarke were thirty ; Bartol, Cranch, and Dwight, twenty-seven ; while Thoreau was but twenty-three, and W. E. Channing, twenty-two. " The Dial " was therefore a journal of youth, filled with the high hopes and dreams of those who had not tested themselves by long experience or severe trial. This youthfulness gave it the freshness and the courage that made it a new beginning in literature.

V

MARGARET FULLER AS EDITOR OF THE DIAL

THE prospectus of "The Dial: A Magazine for Literature, Philosophy, and Religion" bore date of May 4, 1840. The proposed journal was to be published quarterly, on the first day of January, April, July, and October, each number containing 136 octavo pages, making a yearly volume of 544 pages. The first number was announced for the first day of July, 1840. The prospectus was probably written by George Ripley, and the first paragraph gave a definite statement of its aims : "The purpose of this work is to furnish a medium for the freest expression of thought on the questions which interest earnest minds in every community." This was quite in harmony with the last letter quoted from Emerson above, and might have been written by him. "The pages of this journal," the writer went on to say, "will be filled by contributors who possess little in common but the love of individual freedom and the hope of social progress ; who are united by sympathy of spirit, not by agreement in speculation ; whose faith is in Divine Providence, rather than in human prescription ; whose hearts are more in the future than in the past, and who trust the living soul more than the dead letter. It will endeavor to promote the constant evolution of truth, not the petrifaction of opinion. . . . In literature it will strive to exercise a just and catholic criticism, and to recognize every sincere production of genius ; in philosophy it will attempt the reconciliation of the universal instincts of humanity with the largest conclusions of reason ; and in religion it will reverently seek to discover the presence of God in nature, in history, and in the soul of man."

During the first two years of its publication "The Dial" was edited by Margaret Fuller. She was assisted by George Ripley, who was to have oversight of its business management. His connection with it was very slight, however, after his going to Brook Farm in the spring of 1841. The real task of editing the journal fell upon Margaret Fuller, and she was obliged to see that its pages were filled. She was at this time living in Jamaica Plain, a part of the town of Roxbury, and now included in the city of Boston. She had, in November, 1839, begun her conversations in Boston, and in March, 1841, men were admitted to them. They were continued until 1844, when she went to New York to assist Horace Greeley as literary editor of "The Tribune." Of "The Dial" contributors who attended her conversations in 1841 were Ripley, Emerson, Alcott, Hedge, Clarke, Very, Wheeler, Elizabeth Peabody and Mrs. Ripley. The conversations of this year were held at the house of George Ripley, Bedford Place; and a good report of them has been made by Caroline H. Dall, in her little book called "Margaret and Her Friends." Mrs. Dall gives this account of the conversations: "The fame of her talks had spread. She had great need of money, and some of the gentlemen who were accustomed to talk with her, and some of the ladies of her day-class, suggested an evening-class, to be composed of both ladies and gentlemen, and to meet at the house of George Ripley. Ten conversations were to be held, and the tickets of admission cost twenty dollars each, a very high price for that time. . . . The members were full of excitement over the projected opening of Brook Farm. All were in good spirits, and bright sayings ran back and forth."

The "Address of the Editors to the Reader," with which the first number of "The Dial" opened, was written by Emerson. After reading the foregoing correspondence, what he says about the reluctance of the editors in entering upon their

enterprise will be fully appreciated. It will be understood
that a genuine modesty finds expression, when he says :
" Those who have immediately acted in editing the present
number cannot accuse themselves of any unbecoming for-
wardness in their undertaking, but rather of a backwardness,
when they remember how often in many private circles the
work was projected, how eagerly desired, and only postponed
because no individual volunteered to combine and concen-
trate the free-will offerings of many co-operators. With
some reluctance the present conductors of this work have
yielded themselves to the wishes of their friends, finding
something sacred and not to be withstood in the importunity
which urged the production of a journal in a new spirit."
What he says of the revolution going on in society and letters
indicates his own position at that time as one of expectancy
and of desire for radical changes. But still more interesting is his statement as to the sources from which the pages
of the new journal are to be filled : " From the beautiful
recesses of private thought ; from the experience and hope
of spirits which are withdrawing from all old forms, and
seeking in all that is new somewhat to meet their inappeas-
able longings ; from the secret confession of genius afraid to
trust itself to aught but sympathy ; from the conversation
of fervid and mystical pietists ; from tear-stained diaries of
sorrow and passion ; from the manuscripts of young poets ;
and from the records of youthful taste commenting on old
works of art, — we hope to draw thoughts and feelings
which, being alive, can impart life." This is a very different and far more literary statement of the purposes of " The
Dial" than that Emerson gave in the letter already quoted,
and wherein his aim was almost wholly reformatory and
revolutionary. In fact, his idea was many-sided, and had
not reached a state of fixed and dogmatic purpose. " If our
journal share the impulses of the time," he truly said in
his address to the reader, " it cannot now prescribe its own

course. It cannot tell in orderly propositions what it shall attempt. It has all things to say, and no less than all the world for its final audience."

The contributors to the first number of "The Dial" were Margaret Fuller, Emerson, Cranch, Dwight, Ripley, W. H. Channing, Parker, Alcott, and Thoreau. In this number Margaret Fuller had an essay on Criticism, a discussion of Allston's pictures recently on exhibition, and two or three short poems. Ripley contributed a review of the writings of O. A. Brownson. One of Parker's ablest pieces of theological discussion was given to the public in this number, his subject being "The Divine Presence in Nature and the Soul." Alcott furnished selections from his diary, in the form of quotations and brief paragraphs. Cranch provided several poems, as did S. G. Ward. Dwight contributed a short essay that had served as a sermon; and it closed with the only one of his poems that has become widely known. W. H. Channing's contribution was the first part of a theological romance, partly autobiographical. There were also selections from the writings of several members of Emerson's family, already alluded to by him in one of his letters to Carlyle, quoted above. These included a poem by his first wife, Ellen Tucker Emerson. One of the best poems contained in this number was by Mrs. Ellen Hooper. Here Thoreau first appeared in print with a poem entitled "Sympathy," as well as a prose essay.

Immediately after the appearance of the first number, Margaret Fuller wrote to Mrs. Almira Barlow, mother of General Francis C. Barlow: "I have the pleasure of sending you the first number of a periodical some of us, your old friends, are going to scribble in. The introduction is by Mr. Emerson; pieces on Critics and the Allston Gallery by me. The next number will be better." A letter to Emerson, written July 5, indicates fully enough how little satisfied Margaret Fuller was with the first number. Her absence

Introduction to The Dial

while it was passing through the press gave opportunity for
many typographical blunders, some of which must have been
extremely aggravating to the authors in whose articles they
appeared. Other details of the management of the journal
are of interest.

" Until I have seen Mr. R[ipley] I cannot answer all your
questions ; *mais à present,* you can have as many numbers
as you want for yourself or your friends of this first number,
but our contract with them was that twelve numbers should
be given to Mr. R. each quarter, for the use of contributors.
Of these I receive two. Mr. Thoreau will have it, of course,
as we hope his frequent aid. But I did not expect to furnish it to all who may give a piece occasionally. I have not
sent it to E[llen] H[ooper] or C[aroline] S[turgis] or N. I
sent a list to W[eeks] and J[ordan] of those to whom I
wished this number sent. I did not give Mr. Stone's name,
but doubtless Mr. R. did. I will see about it, however. I
presume Mr. Cranch is a subscriber, as is J. F. Clarke, and
others who will write ; but I will look at the list when in
town next Wednesday.

" I desired Mr. Thoreau's ' Persius ' to be sent him, as I
was going away to Cohasset at the time it came out, and I
understood from Mr. R. that it was sent, and he did not
correct it. I do not know how this was ; the errors are most
unhappy. I will not go away again when it is in press.

" I like the poetry better in small type myself and thought
the little page neat and unpretending, but have no such
positive feeling about such things that I would not defer
entirely to your taste. But now we have begun so, I should
think it undesirable to make changes this year, as the first
volume should be uniform. I wish I had consulted you at
first, but did not know you attached great importance to ex-
ternals in such matters, as you do so little in others. The
marks shall be made and the spaces left as you desire, however, after our respective poems.

"I am glad you are not quite dissatisfied with the first number. I feel myself how far it is from that eaglet motion I wanted. I suffer in looking it over now. Did you observe the absurdity of the last two pages? These are things they had to fill up blanks, and which, thinking 't was pity such beautiful thoughts should be lost, they put in for climax. Admire the winding up, the concluding sentence!!

"I agree that Mr. Alcott's sayings read well. I thought to write about the expostulation in your last letter, but finally I think I would rather talk with you.

"The next number we will do far better. I want to open it with your article. You said you might wish to make some alterations if we kept it — do you wish to have it sent you? — the first part is left in type; they had printed a good deal before finding it would be too long. E. H.'s 'Poet,' some of C.'s best, Ellery, and 'The Bard born out of Time,' we must have for that."

"The Bard born out of Time" was a reference to Emerson's "Woodnotes," the first part of which was printed in the second number of "The Dial." Three poems by Ellen Hooper appeared in that number, one of them being entitled "The Poet." Emerson brought together in the same number a collection of the poems of Ellery Channing, under the title of "New Poetry," with appreciative comments. Several poems by Caroline Sturgis (Tappan) appeared in this number.

Writing to Emerson on July 19, Margaret Fuller refers to his lecture on Literature, with which the second number opened. The paragraph criticised by Ripley is at the top of the next to the last page, and was evidently carefully revised by the author, in accordance with these suggestions. This letter also indicates the difficulties under which the editor performed her tasks, especially the limitations put upon her labors by ill-health. She says to Emerson:

"I suppose it is too warm for my dear friend to write, at

least to so dull a correspondent, or perhaps it is that I have
asked so many things. I am sorry you did not send the
verses, for I wanted to take one or two for filling the gaps,
and now have been obliged to take some not so good. Have
you not some distiches to bestow ? I have two or three little
things of yours which I wished very much to use, but thought
I must not without your leave.

"When I wrote the first line of this letter I thought I
should fill it up with some notes I wished to make on the
Hall of Sculpture. But I was obliged to stop by a violent
attack of headache, and now I am not fit to write anything
good, and will only scribble a few lines to send with your
proof which Mr. R. left with me. He is much distressed
with what he thinks a falling off in the end of your paragraph about the majestic artist, and I think when you look
again you will think you have not said what you meant to
say. The 'eloquence' and the 'wealth,' thus grouped have
rather *l'air bourgeois.* 'Saddens and gladdens' is good.
Mr. R. hates prettinesses, as the mistress of a boarding-
house hates flower vases. 'Dreadful melody' does not suit
me. The dreadful has become vulgarized since its natal day.

"So much for impertinence! I am very glad I am to
own these remarks about the Meister. As to the genius of
Goethe, the statement, though so much better than others,
is too imperfect to be true. He requires to be minutely
painted in his own style of hard finish. As he never gave
his soul in a glance, so he cannot be painted at a glance. I
wish this 'Kosmos Beauty' was not here over again. One
does not like their friend to have any way, anything peculiar; he must be too individual to be known by a cough or
a phrase. And is this *costly* true to the sense of *kostliche ?*
that means 'worthy a high price,' the other 'obtained at a
high price,' *n'est-ce pas ?* I cannot like that illustration of
the humors of the eye. I wish the word *whipped* was never
used at all, and here it is twice in nearest neighborhood.

"At this place I was obliged to take to my bed, — my poor
head reminding me that I was in no state for criticism."

Ripley was less pleased with the first number of "The
Dial" than was Margaret Fuller, as may be seen in a letter he wrote to Dwight shortly after its appearance. "You
have seen 'The Dial,' of course," he wrote. "I hope you
like it better than I do. It is quite unworthy, I think, of
its pretensions; and unless the everlasting hills, to which
we have looked for help, give us something more than this,
they had better cease to be parturient." A month later he
wrote again, and with a more cheerful view of the new journal: "How glad I am that you like 'The Dial' so well! and
that the saints in Northampton and Deerfield also have an
eye for its merits. The best judges, though, I think, generally are disappointed. It was not *prononcé* enough.
They expected hoofs and horns, while it proved as gentle
as any sucking dove. The next number, I trust, will make
amends. Still, this has produced a decided sensation. I
feared it would fall dead; but there is no dread of that
now. People seem to look on with wonder; while the
Philistines, who dare show out, are wrathy as fighting-cocks.
Pray send on your articles without delay; and if you have
any more such dainty verses as the last, let them come, too."
How "The Dial" was received by those concerned in its production may be understood from a letter of Mrs. Ripley to
Dwight, soon after the appearance of the first number, even
more fully than from their own correspondence. "We are
heartily rejoiced that you like 'The Dial' well," she wrote,
"George, Margaret, and Theodore [Ripley, Parker, and Miss
Fuller] all run it down unmercifully. It has not fire and
flame enough for them, but the reflected approbation of the
public makes them seem more truly to appreciate it now.
It is thought by many — myself among the number — a
very charming book. Miss Peabody says: 'It is domestic,
giving the every-day state of feeling and thought of the

writers. There is no effort about it, and much strength behind.' The next number will be great. We cannot answer your inquiries with regard to the poetry in 'The Dial,' especially that 'sweet, sad melody' you speak of. Margaret supplies the poetical department from the confidential deposits of private friendship in her portfolio; and we agree not to know the names of the pieces we most admire, that we may always have an answer for those who ask us."

Several of the contributors to "The Dial" have also given their estimate of its worth. In a letter to Margaret Fuller, under date of July 8, in reply to one from her already given, Emerson says of the first number: "Nowhere do I find readers of 'The Dial' poetry, which is my one thing needful in the enterprise. I ask in vain after Z. [Caroline Sturgis], or H. T. [Thoreau], or 'new contributor' [Ellery Channing], — of many a one. They wait till I have done, and then inquire concerning Mr. Parker. I think Alcott's paper of great importance to the journal, inasmuch as otherwise, as far as I have read, there is little that might not appear in any other journal." Writing to her on August 4 he gives his impressions more in detail. " I begin to wish," he says, " to see a different 'Dial' from that which I first imagined. I would not have it too purely literary. I wish we might make a journal so broad and great in the survey that it should lead the opinion of this generation on every great interest, and read the law on property, government, education, as well as on art, letters, and religion. . . . It does not seem worth our while to work with any other than sovereign aims. So I wish we might court some of the good fanatics, and publish chapters on every head in the whole art of living. I am just now turning my pen to scribble and copy on the subjects of Labor, Farm, Reform, Domestic Life, etc., and I ask myself, Why should not 'The Dial' present this homely and grave subject to the men and women of the land ? . . . I know the dangers of such latitude of plan in any but the best-conducted journal. It becomes friendly to special modes of reform; partisan, bigoted, perhaps whimsical; not universal and poetic. But our round-table is not, I fancy, in imminent peril of party and bigotry, and we shall not bruise each the other's whims by the collision." In his diary of the same date he wrote: "I think our 'Dial' ought not to be a mere literary journal, but that the times demand of all a more earnest aim. It ought to contain the best advice on the topics of Government, Temperance, Abolition, Trade, and Domestic Life. It might well add such poetry and sentiment as will now constitute its chief merit. Yet it ought to go straight into life, with the devoted wisdom of the best men and women in the land. It should — should it not? — be a degree nearer to the hodiernal facts than my writings are. I wish to write pure mathematics, and not a culinary almanac or application of science to the arts."

Writing to Carlyle, August 30, Emerson says: "Our community begin to stand in some terror of Transcendentalism, and 'The Dial,' poor little thing, whose first number contains scarce anything considerable or even visible, is just now honored by attacks from almost every newspaper and magazine; which at least betrays the irritability and the instincts of the good public." Writing on September 26, and acknowledging the receipt of the first number, Carlyle says: "Of course I read it with interest; it is an utterance of what is purest, youngest in your land; pure, ethereal, as the voices of the morning! And yet — you know me — for me it is too ethereal, speculative, theoretic." On December 9, he speaks of the second number: "I like it decidedly better than the first; in fact, it is right well worth being put on paper, and sent circulating; I find only, as before, that it is still too much of a soul for circulating as it should. I wish you could in future contrive to mark at the end of each article who writes it, or give me some general key for knowing. I recognize Emerson readily; the rest are οἱ πολλοί for most part. But it is all good and very good as a soul; wants only a body, which want means a great deal! Your paper on 'Literature' is incomparably the worthiest thing hitherto; a thing I read with delight. Speak out, my brave Emerson; there are many good men that listen! Even what you say of Goethe gratifies me; it is one of the few things yet spoken of him from personal insight, the sole kind of things that should be spoken!"

Not even Alcott was pleased with "The Dial." Writing to an English friend on the appearance of the first number, he said: "It is but a twilight 'Dial;'" and to another: "This 'Dial' of ours should have been a truer. It does not content the public, nor even ourselves. Yours, the 'Monthly Magazine' [edited by Heraud], pleases me better in several respects." Writing to Heraud, he declares: "'The Dial' partakes of our vices, it consults the mood and is awed somewhat by the bearing of existing orders, yet is superior to our other literary organs, and satisfies in part the hunger of our youth. It satisfies me not, nor Emerson. It measures not the meridian, but the morning ray; the nations wait for the gnomon that shall mark the broad noon."

How "The Dial" was regarded by those most in sympathy with its purposes is indicated in a personal letter from George P. Bradford. "A considerable part of the time while it was published," he wrote, "I was at Brook Farm. Many of us there hailed its appearance, as it came out from time to time, with great interest; and its coming was an important event to us. With the state of feeling common there it had much that seemed to speak to the condition of many. Some of the little poems were much valued and admired."

It is possible to get some glimpses of what "The Dial" was to those not in the immediate circle of its managers, and these intimations are of value as showing what it was to the public at large. Mrs. Sarah H. Whitman, the poet, and an admirer of Poe, writing from Providence to Orestes A. Brownson, under date of November 19, 1840, has a word to say of the contents of the second number: "You ask me what I think of the poetry of 'The Dial.' I will answer you by referring you to an article called 'New Poetry,' in the last number [being Emerson's notice of the unpublished poems of the younger William E. Channing]. If you have not patience to read it all pray do not forget to read the last piece of poetry quoted therein, beginning, 'Yes, they torment me most exceedingly,' etc. Yet there are beautiful and noble thoughts in this new poetry, though for the most part, very crudely and affectedly expressed. Among the prose articles one of the best is the 'Lesson for the Day' [by Theodore Parker], in the last number."

Another indication of the way in which "The Dial" was regarded may be seen in a letter of Alexander H. Everett, older brother of Edward Everett, who was in 1841 president of Jefferson College in Louisiana, published in the "Life of Brownson." The latter was then editor of the "Boston Quarterly Review," which afterwards became "Brownson's Review." "I see that you have become the organ of Orpheus Alcott," Everett writes to Brownson. "What is the meaning of this? Is 'The Dial' defunct? Does that mysterious Horologue no longer 'repeat the progress of the hour and the day'? I have some doubts, however, whether the presence of Orpheus in the 'Quarterly' will do it much good. Eurydice Fuller, whom you appear to have lost from your pages, was, to my taste, the better contributor of the two. How fares it, in general, with transcendentalism about these times? How are Norton and Ripley carrying on the war? Our faithless chronicles tell us nothing but the price of sugar and coffee."

At least one of "The Dial" writers was thoroughly in sympathy with its spirit, and was ready to accept its performance as admirable. This was William Henry Channing, who was the most romantic and enthusiastic of the transcendentalists. Writing to Margaret Fuller, July 7, 1842, he praised "The Dial" as much as she could have desired. " I like 'The Dial' much," he wrote. " How exquisitely graceful Emerson is ! what a fineness of touch about all he does, and such a genuine appreciation of everything ! I liked his lecture when I heard it [probably that on the Times, with which the first number of the third volume opened], but I had no idea how full it was of manly good sense and humanity and large wisdom. He is dreadfully keen. There are words that go sheer to the very gun-room, blowing up all before them. And the beautiful religion of it all, too. Well, I thank heaven I was born in the same day with him. He has but begun his career. The growth of my honor for him I can count by the hours. This summer, especially, it has shot up like corn after showers. I have no words select enough to symbolize my sense of the delicate, clean-cut, medallion-like nakedness of his poetry. It is quite unique. I was much struck to observe, in reading the extract from Milton in connection with the preceding and succeeding passages of the lecture, how the thoughts and style seemed of one clan, and clad in the same tartan. . . .

" Ellery's verses show the same acute perception in his epithets, descriptive touches, and sometimes movement of the verse that we have always seen in him. . . .

" You are gaining at length, it seems to me, the kind of free, simple, pointed, manly expression which you desire ; and how close and comprehensive your observation is ! But I feel always that the novel would be your true vehicle. To bring out your thought, you need just that variety of character which is always in your mind, but which the essay does not allow. By the by, friend C——, shall the longing of your soul be satisfied, to be one with the Infinite Nature ; but meanwhile serve out your novitiate of humanity. Society is the condition of all sound moral circulation. Plants may breathe oxygen; man wastes on such stimulus. 'Dolon' [by Charles K. Newcomb] is full to crowding with truth and beauty, but alas! it has no keynote for earthly instruments. It is a song made for heaven's harps, sung to the spinet of earth." The C—— referred to was perhaps Charles A. Dana, in his sonnet, entitled "Eternity."

When Parker and his friends came together for holiday recreation, according to John Weiss, "the poetry in 'The Dial' was somewhat lightly treated, and the Orphic sayings [of Alcott] duly venerated." On August 10 Parker and Ripley, with Cranch, visited Emerson, and spent the night in his house. In his journal Parker complained bitterly that Emerson and Ripley spent the whole of the time in talking about "The Dial." "Really it was quite too bad. In our walk, Emerson expressed to me his admiration of —— and his foolish article in 'The Dial.' But, alas! the life is Emerson's, and not ——'s, and so it had been lived before." Writing to Dr. Francis, December 18, Parker said: "'The Dial' bears about the same relation to 'The Boston Quarterly' that Antimachus does to Hercules, Alcott to Brownson, or a band of men and maidens daintily arrayed in finery, walking in a vain show, with kid mitts on their dannies, to a body of stout men in blue frocks, with great arms and hard hands, and legs like the Pillars of Hercules."

It appears from her correspondence that Margaret Fuller did not at any time find the editing of "The Dial" an attractive labor. She needed encouragement from others in order to endure the drudgery with patience. In a letter to Emerson, dated November 7, 1840, she said: "I begin to be much interested in 'The Dial,' finding it brings meat and drink to sundry famishing men and women at a distance from these tables. Meseems you ought to know with what delight 'Woodnotes' have been heard." But in a letter to

W. H. Channing, February 2, 1841, she betrays her need of
sympathy and praise, in order to keep up her courage in the
midst of her task: "Write to me whatever you think about
'The Dial.' I wish very much to get interested in it, and
I can only do so by finding those I love and prize are so.
It is very difficult to me to resolve on publishing any of my
own writing: it never seems worth it, but the topmost
bubble on my life; and the world, the Public! alas! — give
me to realize that there are individuals to whom I can
speak!"

The contributors to "The Dial" not being paid for their
work, they wrote when they wished, and the burden of supplying their deficiencies fell upon the editor. In a letter
written to her mother by Margaret Fuller on Christmas
Day, probably in 1841, she indicates what was required of
her under these circumstances. "I am in a state of extreme
fatigue," she writes; "this is the last week of 'The Dial,'
and, as often happens, the copy did not hold out, and I had
to write in every gap of time. M. and J. [two young
ladies, her pupils] have been writing for me extracts, etc.,
but I have barely scrambled through, and am now quite
unfit to hold a pen." The October number of 1841 contained her long articles on the "Lives of the Great Composers" and "Festus," filling no less than eighty-five pages,
more than one-half the whole. Margaret Fuller drew
upon her note-books in such an emergency, and wrote as
best she could. Some of the articles prepared in this way
have been severely criticised, but by those who did not know
the conditions under which they were produced. That she
could do her best under such circumstances was impossible,
and her style is justly complained of as being slipshod and
uneven. Her critics would not have excelled her in work-
manship had they been compelled to fill fifty or seventy-
five pages quarterly without pay, and at the last moment,
with the printer at the door.

There were other difficulties, as her diary reveals. The contributors were not all to her mind, and she was obliged to publish much that she did not wholly approve. " I wish," she writes in her diary, " I could overcome my distrust of Mr. Alcott's mind." In the same repository of her thoughts she made record concerning her attitude towards Theodore Parker : "He cannot be the leader of my journal, . . . but his learning and just way of thinking will make him a very valuable aid." It was her deliberate theory of what such a journal should be, however, that it should not be restricted by the tastes and preferences of the editor. This policy of hers she has well defined in a letter to Emerson, written November 12, 1843, after she had surrendered the editorship into his hands.

" When I had the care of ' The Dial,' " she wrote to him, " I put in what those connected with me liked, even when it did not well please myself, on this principle, that I considered a magazine was meant to suit more than one class of minds. As I should like to have writings from you, Mr. Ripley, Mr. Parker, etc., so I should like to have writings recommended by each of you. I thought it less important that everything in it should be excellent than that it should represent with some fidelity the state of mind among us, as the name of ' Dial ' said was its intent. So I did not regard your contempt for the long prosa on Transcendentalism — Progress, etc., any more than Parker's disgust at Henry Thoreau's pieces.

" You go on a different principle ; you would have everything in it good according to your taste, which is, in my opinion, though admirable as far as it goes, far too narrow in its range. This is your principle ; very well ! I acquiesce, just as in our intercourse I do not expect you to do what I consider justice to many things I prize.

" I do not care for your not liking the piece, because, when you wrote in your journal that I cared for talent as well as genius, I accepted the words written in dispraise as praise. I wish my tastes and sympathies still more expansive than they are, instead of more severe. Here we differ."

Another difficulty with which the editor of "The Dial" had to contend was the indifferent financial support which it received. One month before the first number was issued Margaret Fuller wrote to Emerson that only thirty subscribers had been secured in Boston. It is probable, therefore, that the first number appeared with not more than one hundred names on the subscription book of "The Dial." The publication of the journal was not well managed, and it suffered many things from those who had it in charge. Its first publishers were Weeks, Jordan & Co., 121 Washington Street, periodical news dealers for the trade, as well as publishers. They were very sanguine of its success, and with high anticipations printed a large number of copies of the earlier numbers. During the second year of the publication they failed, and the extra copies then on hand were distributed among the contributors. With some effort the subscription-list was secured from this firm, and the continued use of the name of the journal was retained only with difficulty. It was proposed to pay Margaret Fuller two hundred dollars for her services as the editor, but as it was not possible to pay the printer, she worked without remuneration.

After the failure of Weeks, Jordan & Co., Elizabeth P. Peabody, then a Boston bookseller and publisher, undertook the task of publication, but with small hope of remuneration for her labors, if any. She had a small book-store in West Street, and was the first person in Boston to sell foreign books and periodicals. She also sold reform works of all kinds, as well as educational and philosophical works. Her store was for many years the headquarters of all persons interested in radical reforms, transcendentalism, Brook

Farm, and especially of the persons outside of Boston, who found that a convenient meeting-place for exchange of ideas.

After Miss Peabody took the publication of "The Dial" in charge she wrote to Emerson that, having paid the printer's bills, she would pay Margaret Fuller first before taking out any commission for her own services, until the editor had received three hundred dollars a year. Then she would take the usual commission for her own services, after which the editor and contributors should receive further compensation. But this letter was written before she had examined the accounts of "The Dial," and when she had done so she wrote of the former publishers as "that rascally firm." Having made an examination of the books of "The Dial," with the aid of a friend [James Freeman Clarke], she found that they did not warrant any pay to the editor, if even so much as the continuation of the journal. In March, 1842, immediately after this examination, Miss Peabody wrote to Emerson that not more than three hundred subscribers could be counted on. She said that if seven hundred and fifty copies were printed, the expenses could not be met, after allowing twenty per cent discount to agents; but if only five hundred copies were printed the expenses could be reduced within the receipts. She also wrote: "Margaret, after knowing these items, decides she cannot give her time to it any more. It is a great care and responsibility, and she is not able to give gratuitous labor. She has gone on in the hope that it might afford her a sufficient compensation to enable her to give up her laborious teaching; but the two labors are altogether too much for her." With this letter went one from Margaret Fuller, in which she announced her decision to discontinue at once her connection with "The Dial."

"I requested Miss Peabody to write to you," she says to Emerson, "but, after looking over her letter, I want to add some lines myself. I hoped they would get at these particulars before you returned from New York, that you might hear them on your way, and not be teased as soon as you arrive at your quiet home, but you came earlier than I expected. Yesterday I found myself so unwell, and really exhausted, while letters received from the family made my stay here so uncertain, that I wrote the little notice with regard to the possibility of suspending 'The Dial' for a time, feeling that I must draw back from any promise that I would see to the summer number; but this morning after J. Clarke and Miss Peabody had at last the means of almost entirely examining the accounts, they give me the result you find in her letter to you, which makes it impossible for me to go on at all.

"I could not do it, in future, if I have the same burden on me as I have had before, even as well as I have done. There is a perceptible diminution of my strength, and this winter has been one of so severe labor I shall not recover fully from it for two or three months. Then, if I must take up a similar course next winter, and have this tie upon me for the summer, I think I should sink under it entirely.

"I grieve to disappoint you after all the trouble you have taken. I am also sorry myself, for if I could have received a maintenance from this 'Dial' I could have done my duties to it well, which I never have all this time, and my time might have been given to my pen; while now, for more than three months, I have been able to write no line except letters. But it cannot be helped. It has been a sad business.

"I think perhaps Mr. Parker would like to carry it on even under these circumstances. For him, or for you, it would be much easier than for me, for you have quiet homes, and better health. Of course, if you do carry it on, I should like to do anything I can to aid you. There must be prompt answer, as the press will wait."

That Margaret Fuller was greatly relieved to be freed

from her editorial task may be seen from a letter written to Emerson after she had gone into the country to rest, and dated from Canton, April 18, 1842. "I received your letter before I left Boston," she wrote, "but in the hurry of the last hours could not write even a notelette with the parcel I requested J. Clarke to make up for you of Borrow, Longfellow, some more shreds of 'Dial,' including the wearifu' Napoleon, and the Prayer Book, if Dorothea Dix could be induced to grant the same. What awkward thing could I have said about your advertisement ? I can't think. All was understood, except that you had said ' I should put my name on the cover and announce myself as editor, only that I am not sure I can bind myself for so long as a year,' and so when I saw the advertisement I was glad, and only so far surprised as that I had not been sure you would do it. How many tedious words !

"I think I shall like being here much and find the rest I need. The country is tolerable, pretty, gentle, unobtrusive — within the house plain kindness, and generally a silence unbroken except by the sounds from the poultry or the wind ; to appreciate which blessing one should have lived half a year in a boarding-house with as infirm a head as mine, and none to ward off interruptions, sick or well."

Margaret Fuller had done her work on "The Dial" as well as it was possible under the limitations imposed upon her. Better health, an adequate salary, paid contributors, would have given her results much superior to those she reached ; but it is doubtful if "The Dial" would have shown a greater literary vigor and freshness. No other periodical of the time published so much that has continued to hold its place in our literature or is likely to survive in the future. Emerson's account of Margaret Fuller's connection with "The Dial" is a generous testimony to the modesty with which she undertook the task, and the skill with which she carried it forward. He speaks of her work as the editor as

being "a private and friendly service." He also speaks of
her unpaid labors as having "made no difference to her ex-
ertion. She put so much heart into it that she bravely
undertook to open, in 'The Dial,' the subjects which most
attracted her ; and she treated, in turn, Goethe and Beet-
hoven, the Rhine and the Romaic Ballads, the Poems of
John Sterling, and several pieces of sentiment, with a spirit
which spared no labor; and when the hard conditions of
journalism held her to an inevitable day, she submitted to
jeoparding a long-cherished subject, by treating it in the
crude and forced article of the month. I remember, after
she had been compelled by ill-health to relinquish the
journal into my hands, my grateful wonder at the facility
with which she assumed the preparation of laborious articles
that might have daunted the most practised scribe."

Margaret Fuller's release from editorial work enabled her
to enter upon the writing of books, for, in the summer of
1843, she made a trip to the lake region, and wrote her
"Summer on the Lakes," the first of her original works.
The essay with which the fourth volume of "The Dial"
opened, called there "The Great Lawsuit," was much enlarged during the next year, and was published in a volume
at the end of 1844, under the title of "Woman in the Nineteenth Century." This was her longest and best work, the
most original and independent ; and it gives the best idea of
her genius. As an interpretation of the nature of woman,
and as a plea for her freedom, it has been surpassed by no
later work. It may be still regarded as the text-book of the
movement for suffrage and larger opportunities for women.
After becoming connected with "The Tribune" she brought
together a number of articles, to which she gave the title of
"Papers on Literature and Art," published in 1846, in two
volumes. In this work were reprinted a number of her contributions to "The Dial," including "A Short Essay on
Critics," "A Record of Impressions produced by the Exhibi-

tion of Mr. Allston's Pictures in the Summer of 1839," " A
Dialogue," which appeared in the first volume ; "Lives of
the Great Composers," in the second volume ; and " The
Modern Drama," in the fourth volume. In 1859, the
" Papers on Literature and Art," were reprinted by Arthur
B. Fuller in one volume, as " Art, Literature, and the
Drama ; " but without change as to contents.

In 1855 Arthur B. Fuller edited " Woman in the Nineteenth Century," adding to it a number of miscellaneous
pieces, and in those were included the dialogue on " Festus "
in the second volume of " The Dial," but reprinted under the
title of " Aglaurion and Laurie." He also edited, in 1859, a
volume of miscellanies, to which he gave the title of " Life
Without and Life Within." In this were reprinted from
the first volume of " The Dial " the article on Meta, now
given the title of " Klopstock and Meta ; " " Magnolia of
Lake Ponchartrain ; " and " Menzel's View of Goethe."
From the second volume were taken a paper on Goethe, and
a translation of Goethe's epilogue to the tragedy of Essex.
A number of pieces contributed to " The Dial " were not
given a place in any of these volumes. These include a
sketch called " Leila," in the first volume ; " Yucca Filamen-
tosa," " Bettine Brentano and her Friend Gunderode," and
" Marie von Oosterwich," in the second volume ; "Enter-
tainments of the Past Winter," " Romaic and Rhine Ballads," and " Canova," in the third volume ; and a brief " Dialogue " near the end of the fourth volume.

It will be seen from this enumeration of what she wrote
for " The Dial," that Margaret Fuller produced nothing
better than what appeared in its pages. She wrote nothing
better in criticism than what she says there about Goethe,
which showed her at her best in that kind of writing. The
essays on the " Great Composers," and on " The Modern
Drama," were as good as anything she produced on their respective subjects, and showed her versatility, as well as her

ambition to comprehend all knowledge. The paper on woman was brilliant with wit and wisdom. Rarely does any journal publish an article so incisive, vigorous, and well reasoned. It need not be said now that all this work was desultory and fragmentary, as was all that Margaret Fuller wrote. She was not an author, but a talker. Brilliant in the highest degree in conversation, pen and paper fettered her genius, which in literature had no adequate expression. She always wrote hastily, under conditions of nervous tension and strain, with no apparent capacity for calm and successful effort. Yet her life was the most romantic and interesting connected with American literature.

VI

EMERSON AS EDITOR OF THE DIAL

EMERSON was much perplexed as to what he ought to do in regard to "The Dial." In the beginning of its publication he had declared his purpose to have no connection with its editing; but he had now become interested in its continuation, and he was not desirous that it should be abandoned. Evidently, he was not willing it should go into the hands of Parker, and those who would make it the organ of reforms in theology and social life. Being very doubtful of what he was willing to undertake in the matter he put down in his diary his thought on the subject. The date of this record is not given, but it followed within a few months after the letter of Margaret Fuller to her brother Richard, written November 5, 1841, in which she said: "I have begun with a smaller class this year than usual, and 'The Dial' is likely to fall through entirely." It was therefore six months before "The Dial" went into the hands of Elizabeth Peabody that its failure was anticipated. Under these circumstances Emerson said in his diary: "'The Dial' is to be sustained or ended; and I must settle the question, it seems, of its life or death. I wish it to live, but I do not wish to be its life. Neither do I like to put it into the hands of the Humanity and Reform men, because they trample on letters and poetry; nor in the hands of the scholars, for they are dead and dry. I do not like the 'Plain Speaker' [an organ of radical reforms] so well as the 'Edinburgh Review.' The spirit of the last may be conventional and artificial, but that of the first is coarse, sour, indigent; dwells in a cellar-kitchen and goes to make suicides." Probably this was written after the receipt of the letters from Elizabeth Peabody and Margaret Fuller announcing the latter's withdrawal from "The Dial." In a letter to Dr. Hedge Emerson more fully expresses his thought in regard to the continuation of the publication. "Poor 'Dial'!" he writes, "it has not pleased any mortal. No man cried, 'God save it!' And yet, though it contains a deal of matter I could gladly spare, I yet value it as a portfolio which preserves and conveys to distant persons precisely what I should borrow and transcribe to send them if I could. It wants mainly and only some devotion on the part of its conductor to it, that it may not be the herbarium that it is of dried flowers, but the vehicle of some living and advancing mind. But nobody has yet conceived himself born for this end only."

In a letter to Margaret Fuller, to which hers from Canton given above is a reply, and dated March 20, 1842, Emerson expresses his decision to continue the publication of "The Dial," and to become its editor. "After thinking a little concerning this matter of 'The Dial,'" he writes, "I incline to undertake it for a time rather than have it stop and go into the hands that know not Joseph. I had rather it should not be suspended. Your friends are my friends, and will give me such aid as they would have given you, and my main resource is to adopt the expedient of selection from old or from foreign books almost with the liberality to which Alcott would carry it, certainly to make Synesius, or Lucian, or Chaucer speak whenever a dull article is offered and rejected. Perhaps I shall rue this day of accepting such an intruder on my peace, such a consumer of my time, as a 'Dial.' Perhaps, then, I shall find some friend of Hercules who will lend a shoulder to uphold the little world. At all events, you have played martyr a little too long alone; let there be rotation in martyrdom. Yet shall you not forget to help. I think also I had rather undertake it alone than with any partnership or oversight such as Mr. Parker or Mr. Ripley, for example. So little skill have I in partnership that I am sure that we should make each other mutually unhappy. Now I will ask of them their whole aid and furtherance. So I think you shall withhold your notice to subscribers, and I will immediately consult Fabricius on Authors for solid condiment to fill up July withal. You will see at once what folios of information on details and good advice for my first adventure I need. Send me word that your head aches less with such prospect of present relief, and we will hope that our 'Dial' will one day grow so rich as to pay its old debts."

From Emerson's letters to Carlyle we learn something more in regard to his purpose in becoming the editor of "The Dial." In writing to Emerson, November 19, 1841, at the time when it had become possible that "The Dial" would be discontinued, Carlyle had expressed his want of interest in it, and even his contempt for its transcendentalisms. "'The Dial,' too," he writes, "it is all spirit-like, aeriform, aurora-borealis like. Will no angel body himself out of that; no stalwart Yankee man, with color in the cheeks of him, and a coat on his back? These things I say ; and yet, very true, you alone can decide what practical meaning is in them." It is quite possible Emerson had in mind this call for a robust man to edit "The Dial" when he undertook that task. In writing to Carlyle, March 31, 1842, Emerson is moved to defend Margaret Fuller and the career of "The Dial ;" and, what is more important, he sets forth his own reasons for undertaking its editorship. "I should tell you," he says, "that my friend Margaret Fuller, who has edited our little 'Dial' with such dubious approbation on the part of you and other men, has suddenly decided a few days ago that she will edit it no more. The second volume was just closing; shall it live for a third year? You should know that, if its interior and spiritual life has been ill fed, its outward and bibliopolic existence has been worse managed. Its publishers failed, its short list of subscribers became shorter, and it has never paid its laborious editor, who has been very generous of her time and labor, the smallest remuneration. Unhappily, to me alone could the question be put whether the little aspiring starveling should be reprieved for another year. I had not the cruelty to kill it, and so must answer with my own proper care and nursing for its new life. Perhaps it is a great folly in me, who have little adroitness in turning off work, to assume this sure vexation, but 'The Dial' has certain charms to me as an opportunity, which I grudge to destroy. Lately at New York I found it to be to a certain class of men and women, though few, an object of tenderness and religion. You cannot believe it?"

"I submitted," says Emerson in a letter to Carlyle written July 1, "to what seemed a necessity of petty literary patriotism, — I know not what else to call it, — and took charge of our thankless little 'Dial,' here, without subscribers enough to pay even a publisher, much less any laborer; it has no penny for editor or contributor, nothing but abuse in the newspapers, or, at best, silence; but it serves as a sort of portfolio, to carry about a few poems or sentences which would otherwise be transcribed and circulated; and always we are waiting when somebody shall come and make it good. But I took it, as I said, and it took me, and a great deal of good time, to a small purpose. I am ashamed to compute how many hours and days these chores consume for me. I had it fully in my heart to write at large leisure in noble mornings opened by prayer or by readings of Plato or whomsoever else is dearest to the Morning Muse, a chapter on Poetry, for which all readings, all studies, are but preparation; but now it is July, and my chapter is in rudest beginnings."

Such were Emerson's regrets that his time should be consumed by editorial drudgery; but he undertook the task with conviction of its desirability, and he held to it without flinching so long as there was any promise that the work could be fortunately continued. He made endeavor to secure the aid of Carlyle, but that genius was not in sympathy with " The Dial," however much he might read it, as he evidently did, from his many references to it. "Thanks for asking me to write you a word in ' The Dial,'" he says in his letter of August 29, 1842. "Had such a purpose struck me long ago, there have been many things passing through my head, some one of which, snatched out of the ragged rank, and dressed and drilled a little, might perhaps fitly have been saved from Chaos, and sent to ' The Dial.' In future we shall be on the outlook. I love your ' Dial,' yet it is with a kind of shudder. You seem to me in danger of dividing yourselves from the Fact of this present Universe, in which alone, ugly as it is, I find any anchorage, and soaring away after Ideas, Beliefs, Revelations, and such like, — into perilous altitudes, as I think." To this Emerson replied, October 15, and reveals the situation in New England amongst that class of persons to whom "The Dial" made appeal. "For 'The Dial' and its sins," he says, "I have no defence to set up. We write as we can, and we know very little about it. If the direction of these speculations is to be deplored, it is yet a fact for literary history that all the bright boys and girls in New England, quite ignorant of each other, take the world so, and come and make confession to fathers and mothers, — the boys that they do not wish to go into trade, the girls that they do not like morning calls and evening parties. They are all religious, but hate the churches; they reject all the ways of living of other men, but have none to offer in their stead. Perhaps, one of these days, a great Yankee shall come, who will easily do the unknown deed."

Elizabeth Peabody gave to the publication of "The Dial" devoted interest and labor. She and her aged father themselves wrapped the numbers for mailing, in order to save expense, and she gave much of her time in other ways, in order that it might be continued. The number for April, 1842, appeared with her name as the publisher, and on the third page of the cover was printed an appeal to the readers to sustain the periodical more faithfully. Prompt payment of the subscription was asked, and that those who bought single numbers should become regular subscribers, in order that a more certain calculation might be made of the number of copies to be printed. On the third page of the cover of the July number, 1842, it was announced that, " with this number, 'The Dial' passes under the editorial care of R. W. Emerson, Concord, Mass., to whom all that concerns the literary department must be addressed." With the October number Emerson's name appeared at the top of the third page of the cover as editor, and there it remained to the end.

The change in editor did not increase the subscription list of " The Dial." In June, 1842, when Emerson was editing the first number brought out under his care, Miss Peabody wrote him that not one-half the copies printed went to regular subscribers; and Emerson himself mentions the exact number as two hundred and twenty. Charles Lane and Henry Thoreau devoted a number of weeks each to canvassing for subscribers, but with little success ; and Horace Greeley largely advertised " The Dial " in the New York " Tribune," gratuitously. In February, 1843, Elizabeth Peabody wrote to Emerson: "Little as 'The Dial' is subscribed for, it is very extra lively read ; " but at the same time she announced that the subscription list was falling off. Emerson not only acted as the editor, but also as the banker of " The Dial." He was obliged to endorse Miss Peabody's notes for its current expenses, and when the publication went into the hands of James Munroe & Co., at the end of the third year, she notified him that she might require him to pay $120 due on its account. Munroe led Emerson to think that with a more careful business management, and in connection with his own publishing business, "The Dial" could be made to succeed. It was therefore put into his hands; but the subscription list did not increase, while the expenses did. Munroe charged one-third of the selling price for its management, and the result was the abandonment of the publication at the end of a year under his control. The book-publishing firm of James Munroe & Co. was located at 134 Washington Street, opposite the Old Corner Book-Store. This house published the earlier works of Emerson, Thoreau, Ellery Channing, and Ripley's Select Library. Its store was for many years a gathering place for the literary men of Boston, who there discussed books, philosophy, religion, and the topics of the day. At one time the firm bore the name of Munroe and Francis. Charles S. Francis located in the publishing business in New York, and brought out the works of Channing, Dewey, Bellows, William Ware, and other Unitarians. He was also the publisher of Audubon's great work.

Emerson's connection with "The Dial" as its editor cost him several hundred dollars, Mr. Sanborn placing the sum definitely at $300. It is not probable that he complained at this expense; at least, there is no printed record that he protested. When he saw that it was impossible for "The Dial" to succeed in securing the patronage of what appeared to be its own legitimate public, he gave up the attempt, and brought the publication to its end. In September, 1854, Elizabeth Peabody wrote to Emerson that a large number of copies of "The Dial" were lying in her brother's store in Boston, and asked him what should be done with them. He carried many of them to his own house, stored them in his attic, and distributed them where he thought they were desired or would be appreciated. The last of them were burned or sold to the ragman in 1872.

Emerson's statement to Carlyle that he found a few persons in New York who highly appreciated "The Dial" has already been quoted. Writing of it in the "Memoirs of Margaret Fuller," Emerson said : " Many years after it was brought to a close, Margaret Fuller was surprised in England by very warm testimony to its merits; and, in 1848, the writer of these pages found it holding the same affectionate place in many a private bookshelf in England and Scotland, which it had secured at home. Good or bad, it cost a good deal of precious labor from those who served it, and from Margaret most of all." Writing to Thoreau from England, in 1848, Emerson said : " ' The Dial ' is absurdly well known here. We at home, I think, are always a little ashamed of it, — I am, — and yet here it is spoken of with the utmost gravity, and I do not laugh." In his " Historic Notes of Life and Letters in New England," Emerson also referred to " The Dial" and its editors. He there said it "enjoyed its obscurity for four years. All its papers were unpaid contributions, and it was rather a work of friendship among the narrow circle of students than the organ of any party. Perhaps its writers were its chief readers; yet it contained some noble papers by Margaret Fuller, and some numbers had an exhausting sale because of papers by Theodore Parker." The biographer of Emerson has truly said that " it is much to have uniformly taken the highest tone upon all subjects; and whatever may be said of ' The Dial,' this praise abundantly belongs to it."

In considering the causes of the failure of " The Dial" we ought to remember the circumstances under which it was published. In the most favorable view of it there was but a small public from which it could draw, the transcendentalists not being many in number in 1840. It is doubtful if such a periodical would meet with anything like success even at the present day. No one of its writers was popular, though two or three of them were well known and widely discussed. With the exception of Theodore Parker, no one of them had a large public anxious to read what he might print. Most of the contributions appeared without any indication of the author, even those of Parker being only marked by a " P." However, the names of the authors of the most important articles soon became known, but only to the few who were especially interested. This fact of withholding the names of the contributors must of itself have had the effect to limit interest in the journal. Had they been known, however, it is not at all probable they would have appealed to a growing constituency. The extreme individualism of the transcendentalists, for this is what it was to a large extent, had the effect of creating dissensions in the possible constituency of " The Dial," and of gradually decreasing the number of subscribers. So great were the diversities of opinion that, whatever "The Dial" might have been, it would not have commanded the support of all transcendentalists. Mr. James Elliot Cabot, one of them in his own personal faith, has justly said of them, in this connection : " No two of them precisely agreed as to what they would have." Some of the early friends of " The Dial" withdrew from its support because it proved to have no creed of any kind to support, or, as they said, because it had no definite aim. On the other hand, there were those who thought it too conservative, too much inclined to support the old order of things, and not vigorous enough to act an iconoclastic part. To the extreme idealists like Mr. Alcott it was not idealistic enough, being too mundane and realistic. To the reformers like Mr. Parker it was too superfine and ethereal, had not body and substance enough, and was wanting in power to strike vigorous blows against the wrongs of mankind. Even to Emerson himself, as we have seen, there were limitations enough to have withdrawn him from its support had he not been deeply committed to the interests of a free journal. " Emerson, for his part," as his biographer says " was in favor of the largest liberty and the most extravagant aspirations, but he winced in spite of himself at the violations of literary form, and he confessed, in strict confidence, that he found some of the numbers unreadable." To bring such a company of come-outers, critics, iconoclasts, and extreme individualists, into working harmony with each other proved to be impossible; and this was why "The Dial" lived but four years. In his account of the connection of Margaret Fuller with "The Dial" Emerson stated the real conditions under which it was published, and the causes of its failure. That he should have made such a statement is a testimony to his practical sagacity and to his power of intellectual apprehension.

"She was eagerly solicited," Emerson says of Margaret Fuller, "to undertake the charge of this work, which, when it began, concentrated a good deal of hope and affection. It had its origin in a club of speculative students, who found the air in America getting a little close and stagnant; and the agitation had perhaps the fault of being too secondary or bookish in its origin, or caught not from primary instincts, but from English, and still more from German books. The journal was commenced with much hope, and liberal promises of many co-operators. But the workmen of sufficient culture for a poetical and philosophical magazine were too few; and, as the pages were filled by unpaid contributors, each of whom had, according to the usage and necessity of this country, some paying employment, the journal did not get his best work, but his second best. Its scattered writers had not digested their theories into a distinct dogma, still less into a practical measure which the public could grasp; and the magazine was so eclectic and miscellaneous that each of its readers and writers valued only a small portion of it. For these reasons it never had a large circulation, and it was discontinued after four years. But 'The Dial' betrayed, through all its juvenility, timidity, and conventional rubbish, some sparks of true love and hope, and of the piety to spiritual laws which had moved its friends and founders, and it was received by its early subscribers with almost a religious welcome."

Though but poorly sustained, "The Dial" served an admirable purpose. It enabled the transcendentalists to speak to each other, it brought their philosophy more distinctly before the public, it permitted them to give their thoughts a clearer utterance than they otherwise would have done, and it helped them to realize what their own cause meant to themselves and others. It gave them courage to appeal to the public with what they regarded as a larger and truer conception of life. It was not their aim to write fine essays and learned books, for their movement was not purely literary in its nature. It was religious as well as intellectual, moral rather than literary; and it had in it the prophetic spirit. It was not a new form of inquiry about life and its problems, but it was a regenerating and inspiring impulse, leading men toward "plain living and high thinking." Transcendentalism came like a gospel to those who accepted it. None of "The Dial" writers put pen to paper merely as literary artists. First of all, they had a word to utter, and they were anxious to reform the world, to rejuvenate it with their own spirit. In any age such aims, in connection with literature, meet with little appreciation and favor. The best service performed by "The Dial," however, was to stimulate a considerable number of persons to express their thoughts on the printed page. In itself this was nothing, but the persons who were influenced proved to have something to say that the world needed to hear. It is probable that Margaret Fuller, Thoreau, and Ellery Channing would have found another way to give their essays and poems to the public, but it is not to be forgotten that "The Dial" first did this service for them.

Introduction to The Dial

That which induced Emerson to devote time and money to "The Dial" was that it afforded an opportunity for several of his young friends and protégés to reach the public. Limited as was its circulation, it enabled Alcott, Thoreau, Channing, Newcomb, and others, to appear in print, and to appeal to those who were in need of their message. Writing to Margaret Fuller, March 30, 1840, while "The Dial" was yet a thing of the future, he said : "Were I responsible, I would rather trust for its wit and its verses to the eight or nine persons in whose affections I have a secure place than to eighty or ninety celebrated contributors." It will be seen hereafter to what an extent "The Dial" was managed in accordance with this declaration of purpose, and how many of its contributors were induced to write for it or to permit the publication in its pages of their verses or sketches at the earnest solicitation of Emerson. The letter of Mrs. George Ripley to John S. Dwight has already indicated that Margaret Fuller pursued the same method, and that she filled many a page with contributions solicited from young friends she wished to encourage and to make known to the public "The Dial" afforded them. Emerson wished that the journal should be especially devoted to poetry, and to that which was written from inward necessity and not with a merely literary motif. On the appearance of the first number he complained to Margaret Fuller that the verse was not made more prominent by the use of larger type. He wished to have everything considered from the poetical point of view, and looked upon, as he said, "at large angles."

It is difficult to understand the limited circulation of "The Dial" when it is considered how largely Emerson contributed to its pages. To the first volume he contributed six poems that were reprinted in his "Poems" of 1847, his first poetical volume. These were "To . . . [Eva]," "The Problem," "Woodnotes," "The Snow Storm," "Suum

102

Cuique," "The Sphinx." These include at least four of his best poems, and that are most widely known. In writing to Emerson in preparation for the second number of "The Dial," Margaret Fuller begged him to send her some verses "for filling the gaps." For this purpose she secured and used a little poem of six lines, which appeared under the title of "Silence," at the end of Emerson's paper on "Modern Literature." It was not reprinted until the revised edition of the "Poems," in 1883, in which it appears on page 300 as "Eros." "In regard to my own verses," Emerson wrote to Rufus W. Griswold, September 25, 1841, when five numbers of "The Dial" had been published, "I have printed them all either in 'The Western Messenger,' in the same number which contained 'The Humble-Bee,' or the two or three following numbers, where they appeared with my name, — or in 'The Dial.' As I do not happen to have in the house a copy of either of these journals, I can only indicate those which I remember in 'The Dial.' They are 'The Problem;' Stanzas — 'O fair and stately maid, whose eye,' etc. ; 'Suum Cuique;' 'The Snow Storm;' 'The Sphinx;' 'Woodnotes, No. I.;' and 'Woodnotes, No. II.,' which appears in the forthcoming number for October, with a little piece called 'Fate,' and another 'Painting and Sculpture.' There may be more than these few, but I do not remember them." It will be seen that he omitted "Silence" and "To Eva." Besides the introductory "Address of the Editors to the Reader," Emerson contributed to the first volume of "The Dial" three of his lectures. These were "Thoughts on Modern Literature," which was reprinted in "The Natural History of the Intellect and Other Papers;" "Thoughts on Art," reprinted as "Art" in "Society and Solitude;" and "Man the Reformer," reprinted in the "Miscellanies" of 1856. In the second number appeared Emerson's article on "New Poetry," an appreciative notice of the then unpublished poetry of Ellery Channing, including a dozen of his poems. This paper has never been reprinted.

To the second volume of "The Dial" Emerson also contributed six poems: "Painting and Sculpture," "Fate," "Woodnotes" (the second part), "The Park," "Forbearance," and "Grace," all of which were reprinted in the "Poems" of 1847. The prose contributions were a paper on Walter Savage Landor, reprinted in "Natural History of the Intellect;" "The Senses and the Soul," not reprinted, though a pamphlet edition of it was edited in England by Walter Lewin, in 1884.

Five of Emerson's poems appeared in the third volume of "The Dial," all reprinted in the "Poems" of 1847. These were "Tact," "Holidays," "The Amulet," "Saadi," and "To Eva [Ellen] at the South." His prose contributions to this volume were no less than eight in number, not counting his many reviews of books and other editorial work. The volume opened with his "Lectures on the Times — Introductory," reprinted in the "Miscellanies" of 1856. In the same number also was printed an article entitled "Prayers," which was compiled from papers sent him by friends. It was reprinted in the "Natural History of the Intellect." The selections from the "Veeshnoo Sarma" were made by Emerson, and this was perhaps the first time that the "Bibles of the East" were offered to readers in this country in an accessible form. This paper was followed by several others of a like nature, some of them prepared by Thoreau. In this way Emerson manifested his keen interest in the great religious books of Oriental lands, and his conviction that they are worthy of general recognition. A paper on "Fourierism and the Socialists" has not been reprinted. That on "The Chardon Street and Bible Conventions" was reprinted in the "Lectures" of 1883. The one on the "Agriculture of Massachusetts" was reprinted in the "Natural History of the Intellect." It will be seen, therefore, that Emerson printed three poems and six prose papers in the first number of "The Dial" edited by him. In the same volume appeared "The Conservative," reprinted in the "Miscellanies" of 1856; "English Reformers" not reprinted; and "The Transcendentalist," reprinted in the "Miscellanies" of 1856.

The fourth volume of "The Dial" also contained six of Emerson's poems. Those entitled "To Rhea," "Ode to Beauty," "Eros," and "The Visit" were reprinted in the "Poems" of 1847. "Gifts" has not been reprinted. "The Times — a Fragment" was reprinted in the "Poems" of 1883. There is some authority for attributing "The Three Dimensions," in the second number to him. Of the six prose contributions the lecture on "The Young American" was reprinted in the "Miscellanies" of 1856, and that on "The Comic" in "Letters and Social Aims." A paper called "Tantalus" was reprinted in the third volume of the Riverside edition of 1883, that entitled "Nature." Papers called "Past and Present," "A Letter," and "The Tragic," were reprinted in "Natural History of the Intellect." The amount of Emerson's work in the way of literary notices was also very considerable. In the first volume he reviewed Dana's "Two Years before the Mast," and with keener interest because Dana was a pupil of his in Cambridge. In a letter to his brother William he said the book was as good as Robinson Crusoe, "and all true. He was my scholar once, but he never learned this of me, more's the pity." In the same number he reviewed Albert Brisbane's "Social Destiny of Man," a condensed presentation of the social system of Fourier. In the second volume he commended Jones Very's "Essays and Poems," the genius of which, he said, "reaches an extraordinary depth of sentiment." In his book reviews he ranged widely in his appreciations. He noticed the poems of Wordsworth, Tennyson, Browning, Ellery

Channing, and others; and he had a word to say of "Europe and European Books" (reprinted in the "Natural History of the Intellect"); as well as of the works of Borrow and the death of Dr. Channing. Truly, "The Dial" took a great deal of Emerson's time to small purpose; and we may say without hesitation that he was not the man for such tasks.

In "The Literary World," of Boston, in 1879, George William Curtis gave an admirable statement of the relations of Emerson to "The Dial," and of the influence it exerted upon the literary development of the country. It is an appreciative and yet a just estimate of the transcendental movement and of its literary organ.

"To speak of 'The Dial' is to recall one of those products of the 'transcendental' epoch which seem to those who look back upon them like 'golden exhalations of the dawn.' Brook Farm, 'The Dial' the active interest in German literature and philosophy and music, Theodore Parker's preaching, were all signs then, as they are traditions now, of the general moral and intellectual revival to which also the impetus of the Anti-Slavery crusade and of the Woman's Rights agitation belongs. 'The Dial,' while not an organ of any particular movement, was the literary gazette of the 'new spirit,' and its natural editor was Mr. Emerson, whose serene genius and temperament, with his commanding and poetic public discourses, and the dignity, simplicity, and purity of his life, had made him the peculiar representative of 'Transcendentalism.' It was his only service as an editor, in the usual sense, and the labor was not exclusively his. It was understood that Mr. Emerson and Miss Margaret Fuller were the editorial council, and in the opening address of 'The Editors to the Reader' Mr. Emerson speaks modestly of 'those who have immediately acted in editing the present number,' in a tone which implies that it was wholly a labor of love.

"The first number of 'The Dial' was issued forty years

ago, in July, 1840, and it is still a most interesting and remarkable publication. There had been nothing like it in this country, and if Schiller's *Horen* may have aimed as high, there were not the same favoring circumstances; so that 'The Dial' remains unique in periodical literature. Its purpose was the most various expression of the best, the most cultivated, and the freest thought of the time, and it was addressed to those only who were able to find 'entertainment' in such literature. There were no baits for popularity. In the modern familiar phrase each number was a symposium of the most accomplished minds in the country. But its circle both of contributors and of readers was local and small. The first number was made up of papers by Mr. Emerson and Miss Fuller, Theodore Parker, George Ripley, William H. Channing, John S. Dwight, A. Bronson Alcott, and Dr. Hedge, — I believe, — with passages from the journal of Charles Chauncy Emerson, to whose memory Dr. Holmes paid so beautiful a tribute in his 'Metrical Essay.' The poetry of the number was supplied by Mr. Emerson, Mr. Cranch, Miss Fuller, Mr. Dwight, Edward Emerson, Henry Thoreau, and Mrs. Hooper. It was almost wholly a 'Boston book,' but it is a part of our literature. Among its memorable contributions was Mr. Emerson's poem 'The Problem,' with its line which is now like Shakespeare's famous lines, a universal expression, —

'He builded better than he knew;'

and his exquisite song, —

'O fair and stately maid!'

to which may be fitly applied his own words in the next number of 'The Dial,' when speaking of Ellery Channing's poetry, that it 'is of such extreme beauty that we do not remember anything more perfect of its kind. Had the poet been looking over a book of Raffaelle's drawings, or perchance the villas and temples of Palladio, with the maiden to whom it was addressed?'

"'The Dial' was published for four years, and it truly marked the transcendental time of day. It is the memorial of an intellectual impulse which the national life has never lost. 'Many readers,' as Mr. Emerson said in his preface to the first edition of Carlyle's collected essays, 'will here find pages which in the scattered anonymous sheets of the —— magazine spoke to their youthful mind with an emphasis that hindered them from sleep.'

"The influence of its editor has been noiseless but extraordinary. Many of the most popular and immediately effective American writers and orators seem to have been middlemen between Mr. Emerson and the great public. To the young men of the last generation he spoke with the same deep power with which Dr. Channing affected Mr. Emerson's own younger generation; and that power he has never lost, because he has always reverenced the dreams of his youth. Those who have felt throughout their lives this purifying and elevating and liberalizing power, and who have seen in his inspiring career the perfect sanity of true genius, can never think without affectionate reverence of Ralph Waldo Emerson."

VII

THE RIPLEYS

GEORGE RIPLEY wrote the article on "Brownson's Writings" published in the first number of "The Dial," and also the "Letter to a Theological Student" in the second number. Many of the review articles were probably from his pen, and all of those not credited to Margaret Fuller or Emerson in the first volume may be regarded as his. It is impossible now to identify all of them, but he is likely to have rendered much help in this direction, at first. The opening of Brook Farm nine months after the first number of "The Dial" was issued, withdrew him from as active a part in its management as would have been his had he remained in his pulpit. Therefore it is difficult to say how much he wrote for it, in addition to the two articles already named.

George Ripley was born in Greenfield, Mass., October 3, 1802, graduated from Harvard in 1823, and from the Divinity School in 1826. In the last year he was settled over the Purchase Street Church in Boston. He was active in planning "The Dial," and he was one of those most desirous that the transcendentalists should have an organ of their own. He had very early made himself master of the German language, and no one gave more zealous attention to the leaders of philosophical thought in Germany. His "Discourses on the Philosophy of Religion Addressed to Doubters who wish to Believe," published in 1836, was one of the first systematic statements of idealism coming from any American pulpit. The "Specimens of Foreign Standard Literature," begun in 1838, first made the German and French thinkers familiar to American readers. He planned

that this series should include a much larger number of
works than actually appeared in it, for his prospectus gave
the names of Fichte, Richter, Herder, Schelling, Schleiermacher, Lessing, Jacobi, Novalis, and others, as amongst
those whose works were to appear in its succeeding volumes. In 1839 he made a vigorous defence of transcendentalism in his controversy with Andrews Norton, the
leading Unitarian theologian at that time. Under the
signature of "An Alumnus" he addressed three letters to
that Divinity School professor, setting forth the teachings
of the leading German theologians, as well as his own
affirmative ideas.

After being settled over the Purchase Street Church from
1826 to 1840, Ripley withdrew from the Unitarian ministry.
About April 1, 1841, he went to Brook Farm, and was at
the head of that institution until the summer of 1847. "The
Harbinger" was begun at Brook Farm June 14, 1845, with
Ripley and Dwight as the editors. It was a weekly of sixteen pages, three columns to the page. Though small in
size, it was ably edited, and had a remarkable corps of contributors. Few journals have ever been published in this
country that have shown equal intellectual and literary
ability. The organ of the teachings of the French socialist
Fourier, it discussed a wide range of subjects, — reformatory, social, musical and artistic, literary, philosophical,
and practical. Many of the "Dial" contributors also wrote
for it, including Hedge, Clarke, Lowell, W. E. Channing,
W. H. Channing, Cranch, C. A. Dana, and Curtis. Other
writers were Whittier, Greeley, Godwin, Brisbane, Higginson, Story, Lazarus, Calvert, Henry James, and Francis
George Shaw. It published much good poetry, the first
American translation of "Consuelo," many of the ablest
French socialistic works, some of the best criticisms that
have ever appeared in any American journal, the first really
valuable appreciations of musical works published in this

country, ably discussed all the social problems of that day, and was, in a word, the only really important socialist journal that has ever been published in the United States. The last number of "The Harbinger" issued at Brook Farm was that of October 30, 1847. It was then transferred to New York, and was continued until February 10, 1849. It had an able corps of writers, and every effort was made to sustain it; but, though it was enlarged, it appealed to a rapidly diminishing constituency. The associationist movement culminated at this time, and interest in it rapidly waned, owing to the failure of the many communities that had been organized throughout the country. Though the associationists, as they called themselves, kept up an organization for a few years longer, the whole movement had come to an end before the beginning of the civil war. It is quite certain that George Ripley and most of his friends never lost their faith in association, but he was unwilling to write the history of Brook Farm, as he was often urged to do by those who appreciated that unique social experiment.

In 1849 Ripley became connected with the New York "Tribune" as literary editor and critic, and his work on that journal was of great importance. From 1857 to 1862 he edited, with Charles A. Dana, the "New American Cyclopedia." He did other editorial work, all of it of high merit and sound critical skill. His ripe scholarship, judicial and appreciative tone of mind, and high moral conviction, were characteristic of his contributions to "The Dial" as to "The Harbinger" and "The Tribune." It was characteristic of Ripley that he should say in his "Letter to a Theological Student," "No man can preach well unless he coin his own flesh and blood, the living, palpitating fibres of his very heart, into the words which he utters from the pulpit. If he speak what he has learned from others, what he finds in books, what he thinks is decorous and seemly that he should say in his place, he may indeed be a good mechanic in the pulpit, he may help to hand down a worm-eaten, stereotyped system of theology, to those who have no more heart for it than he has himself; but a true prophet of God, a man baptized with the Holy Ghost and with fire he can never be." Although these words were written three years before Ripley left the pulpit, they will, in a measure, account for his doing so, as they also help to interpret the attitude of the transcendentalists towards religion.

George Ripley was one of the earliest and most consistent of the transcendentalists. He was one of the first persons in this country to definitely state, in philosophical terms, the principles of idealism, and to defend them with skill and learning. In "The Christian Examiner" for November, 1836, he published an able review of Martineau's "Rationale of Religious Enquiry." In that article he said: "The first step in the proof of supernatural inspiration is the admission of natural inspiration. The foundation for this is laid in the primitive elements of our being. The power of the soul, by which it gains the intuitive perception of spiritual truth, is the original inspiration that forms the common endowment of human nature. This, we maintain, is established by the testimony of the absolute or intuitive reason of man. Our own consciousness assures us that a revelation of great spiritual truths is made to the soul. There are certain primitive and fundamental ideas which compose the substance of reason, that exist, with more or less distinctness, in every intelligent mind. These ideas are the primitive perceptions on which all moral and religious truth is founded, just as the whole science of mathematics is built up on a few simple definitions and axioms, which neither require, nor are susceptible of demonstration. These ideas, by the necessity of our nature, we refer to an origin out of ourselves. They are not created by us, but they command us. They are not the products of our own will, but should be its sovereigns. They are not limited to our own personality, but bear the signatures of universal and everlasting authority. Now, psychology and the history of man alike compel us to trace back their origin to God. We are conscious that they do not proceed from any act of volition of the personal causality which acts within us, nor from the influence of nature, the material causality which acts without us; and we are, therefore, compelled by the authority of our reason to refer them to the Absolute Causality, — the Infinite Author of Truth and Good. They do not grow out of any deductions of our understandings, but are the fruits of a spontaneous and original inspiration, without which the understanding would have no materials to work upon."

This article was the occasion of much discussion, and it was replied to with vigor by Andrews Norton, a professor in the Harvard Divinity School, and the leading Unitarian critic in his day. In the course of this discussion Ripley published three thick pamphlets in reply to Norton's aspersions of what he called "the latest form of infidelity." Ripley especially objected to the mechanical interpretation of the miracles of Christ, holding them to be manifestations of his personal power, expressions of his transcendent spiritual genius. Norton objected to this explanation, and maintained that Christianity has no meaning apart from the miracles as objective phenomena. Ripley's contention was that the miracles of Christ "were the free expression of his character, rather than the formal supports of his mission." His transcendentalism caused him to say that "miracles do not compose the essence of the Christian revelation." He also declared that "a firm faith in Christianity may be cherished independently of miracles." Although this proposition had been maintained by several of the leading English theologians in the seventeenth century, yet it was vigorously combated here, even on the part of Unitarians like Professor Norton.

In his discourses on the philosophy of religion, preached in his church during the year 1834, although they were not published until 1836, Ripley gave an affirmative interpretation of his transcendentalism, as applied to Christianity. His fifth sermon was on the coincidence of Christianity with the higher nature of man. "If there is any created thing," he says, "which displays the seal of Divinity, and bears the impress upon its face that it comes from God, it is the higher nature of man — the faculties of Reason and Conscience, — the power of conceiving and aspiring after Divine Perfection." His claim is that "the dictates of Christianity and the dictates of our higher nature are identical;" and again: "The divine message of the Gospel corresponds to the divine instincts of the soul. It explains and strengthens them." The medium through which the higher nature manifests itself is reason, which Ripley maintains is "the faculty of perceiving primitive, spiritual truth." He regards reason as the very essence of the soul, and says "it gives the immediate perception of truth." It is to reason, conscience, love, and the desire for perfection, that we are to look for what is primitive and genuine in man; and all of them bring man into direct connection with God and his ultimate truths. He says of the soul, in its relation to these spiritual faculties: "It found itself in possession of them, when it first awoke to a full consciousness of its own nature, and felt itself impelled by a resistless force to manifest and exercise them. They can be traced to no other source than to the Eternal Fountain of Truth and Good." "The decisions of Reason," he declares, "which may be regarded as the very essence of the soul, compel us to admit the existence of God as the ground of our own existence, of an Infinite Being as the first cause of finite nature, of an invisible spirit as the origin and support of the visible universe."

In this statement of transcendentalism Ripley was not wholly in agreement with Emerson and Alcott, who put less emphasis upon reason. Emerson put forward the moral faculty as that of the truest revelation of man's higher nature, while Alcott gave the preference to intuition or spiritual insight. He was too much of a theologian to state his faith in a form that was in harmony with these more poetic conceptions of life and its higher experiences. Ripley died in New York, July 4, 1880.

Mrs. Ripley was a "Dial" writer, a short article on "Woman" in the third number being from her pen; and she wrote that on "Painting and Sculpture" in the fifth number, as well as the "Letter from Zoar" contained in the same number. She was Sophia Willard Dana of Cambridge, and was married in 1827. At Brook Farm she taught history and the modern languages with much success, and took a leading part in the management of the school. She thoroughly believed in association, and labored early and late for the success of Brook Farm. In the kitchen and laundry she toiled many hours daily, turning away from the society she adorned and the culture she enjoyed, to become a drudge and skilful manager. O. B. Frothingham said of her that she was "a woman of burning enthusiasm, warm feeling, and passionate will." Theodore Parker wrote of her in his diary: "Mrs. Ripley gave me a tacit rebuke for not shrieking at wrongs, and spoke of the danger of losing our humanity in abstractions." Great indeed must have been her zeal for reforming the world when she could complain of the coldness of Parker, who was being shrieked at on all hands because he was too active in that direction. Mrs. Ripley's article on Woman in "The Dial" was in accord with these interpretations of her character, for it was radical, witty, and vigorous in thought. It took much the same attitude that Margaret Fuller did in her "Woman in the Nineteenth Century," and insisted that a woman should have the right to do what she can do best, all barriers being removed, and she being trusted to judge for herself what is fitted to her nature and to her needs.

After leaving Brook Farm the Ripleys removed to Flatbush, Long Island, where they lived for two years before moving to New York City.   Here Mrs. Ripley taught school in order to add to the family income.   During this time she was gradually drawn to the Catholic Church, of which she became a member in 1849.   She devoted herself more ardently and unreservedly to Brook Farm than any other member, and the reaction produced by its failure carried her to the other extreme.

VIII

THOREAU AS CONTRIBUTOR AND ASSISTANT EDITOR

To the first number of "The Dial" Thoreau contributed a poem and a prose article, and to the third a poem. His first poem in "The Dial," which appeared in the first number, was his earliest contribution of any importance to appear in print. It was his "Sympathy," in the measure of Davenant's "Gondibert," and shows his familiarity with Elizabethan literature. This poem, as well as his "To the Maiden in the East," and several sonnets as yet unpublished, are said to have been addressed to Ellen Sewall, who was loved by Thoreau and his brother John. Thoreau silently gave preference to his brother; but the loved one married another. This story, sanctioned by Emerson, would have it that the gentle boy of the poem is a beautiful maiden; but another version says the boy was a brother of Miss Sewall, who much resembled her, and who was of a most lovable disposition and great promise. The other contribution to the first number of "The Dial" was based on his readings of the satires of Persius, and was, in his own words, his "first printed paper of consequence." This article had the effect of bringing him the friendship of Harrison G. O. Blake, his literary executor, and the editor of four volumes from his diaries. "My first real introduction," says Mr. Blake, "was from the reading of an article of his in 'The Dial' on Aulus Persius Flaccus, which appears now in 'A Week.' That led to my first writing to him, and to his reply, which is printed in the volume of letters. Our correspondence continued for more than twelve years, and we visited each other at times, he coming here to Worcester, commonly to read something in public, or being on his way to read something elsewhere."

In the third number of " The Dial " appeared a poem on Nature from the pen of Thoreau, but printed with the title of " Stanzas." This poem was incorporated into " A Week," but is not one of his best. To the second volume of " The Dial," however, Thoreau contributed two of his most notable poems. The first of these was " Sic Vita," which also found a place in " A Week." The other was printed as " Friendship," was included in " A Week," but when appended to " Letters to Various Persons " was given the title of " Friends, Romans, Countrymen, and Lovers." " Sic Vita" was written on a sheet of paper, and this was wrapped around a bunch of violets, tied together loosely with a straw, that was thrown into the window of a friend. Mr. Alcott read it at Thoreau's funeral as an appropriate expression of his life.

The year 1841, when Thoreau was twenty-six years of age, was that of his greatest poetical activity. Nearly all his poems were written at that time. Writing in the autumn of that year, he said : " Just now I am in the mid-sea of verses, and they actually rustle round me, as the leaves would round the head of Autumnus himself, should he thrust it up through some vales which I know ; but, alas ! many of them are but crisped and yellow leaves like his, I fear, and will deserve no better fate than to make mould for new harvests." His poems were written in a large blank book, and this was drawn upon when Emerson wished to fill some of the pages of " The Dial" with them. After 1843 he wrote few poems, and most of those actually produced he destroyed, an act he regretted in later years. He destroyed them because of Emerson's criticism; but in time Thoreau came to think his own judgment was wiser than that of his friend, an opinion now shared by all of Thoreau's admirers. Most of his poems he gave a place in his prose works, for which many of them were written.

That Thoreau did not write more for " The Dial " as edited
by Margaret Fuller is to be explained by their correspondence. From that it will be seen that he met with the fate
of having his work rejected, but with a long explanation of
why it was not accepted. A poem written in 1841 or at
about that time, and addressed to Wachusett, Monadnock,
and the other hills he could see from Concord, to be found
near the beginning of " A Walk to Wachusett," in " Excursions," was sent to Margaret Fuller ; and the good advice she
sent him instead of printing his poem is worth reading. " I
do not find the poem on the mountains improved by mere
compression," she wrote, " though it might be by fusion and
glow. Its merits to me are, a noble recognition of nature,
two or three manly thoughts, and, in one place, a plaintive
music. The image of the ships does not please me origi-
nally. It illustrates the greater by the less, and affects me
as when Byron compares the light on Jura to that of the
dark eye of woman. I cannot define my position here, and
a large class of readers would differ from me. As the poet
goes on to say —

> ' Unhewn primeval timber,
> For knees so stiff, for masts so limber,'

he seems to chase an image, already rather forced, into
conceits.

" Yet now that I have some knowledge of the man, it
seems there is no objection I could make to his lines (with
the exception of such offences against taste as the lines
about the humors of the eye, as to which we are already
agreed) which I would not make to himself. He is healthful, rare, of open eye, ready hand, and noble scope. He sets
no limit to his life, nor to the invasions of nature ; he is
not wilfully pragmatical, cautious, ascetic, or fantastical.
But he is as yet a somewhat bare hill, which the warm
gales of spring have not visited. Thought lies too detached,
truth is seen too much in detail ; we can number and mark

the substance imbedded in the rock. Thus his verses are startling as much as stern ; the thought does not excuse its conscious existence by letting us see its relation with life; there is want of fluent music. Yet what could a companion do at present, unless to tame the guardian of the Alps too early ? Leave him at peace amid his native snows. He is friendly ; he will find the generous office that shall educate him. It is not a soil for the citron and the rose, but for the whortleberry, the pine, or the heather.

" The unfolding of affections, a wider and deeper human experience, the harmonizing influence of other natures, will mould the man and melt his verse. He will seek thought less and find knowledge the more. I can have no advice or criticism for a person so sincere ; but, if I give my impression of him, I will say, ' He says too constantly of Nature, she is mine.' She is not yours till you have been more hers. Seek the lotus, and take a draught of rapture. Say not so confidently all places, all occasions are alike. This will never come true till you have found it false.

" I do not know that I have more to say now ; perhaps these words will say nothing to you. If intercourse shall continue, perhaps a bridge may be made between two minds so widely apart ; for I apprehend you in spirit, and you do not seem to mistake me so widely as most of your kind do. If you should find yourself inclined to write to me, as you thought you might, I dare say many thoughts would be suggested to me ; many have already, by seeing you from day to day. Will you finish the poem in your own way, and send it for ' The Dial ' ? Leave out —

'And seem to milk the sky.'

The image is too low ; Mr. Emerson thought so too.

"Farewell! May truth be irradiated by Beauty ! Let me know whether you go to the lonely hut [the Hollowell Place in Concord], and write to me about Shakespeare, if you read him there. I have many thoughts about him, which I have never yet been led to express.

"The pencilled paper Mr. E. put into my hands. I have taken the liberty to copy it. You expressed one day my opinion, — that the moment such a crisis is passed, we may speak of it. There is no need of artificial delicacy, of secrecy; it keeps its own secrets; it cannot be made false. Thus you will not be sorry that I have seen the paper. Will you not send me some other records of the *good week* ?"

As soon as Emerson was editor of "The Dial" Thoreau became a frequent contributor, furnishing sixteen poems, prose articles, and other contributions to the third volume, and eight to the fourth. It was in order that he might furnish an opportunity for Thoreau, Ellery Channing, Alcott, and other friends, to reach the public that Emerson undertook the editorship. By this act of friendship Thoreau profited more than any other person, except Ellery Channing, so far as getting into print was concerned. At the same time, Thoreau was an invaluable assistant to Emerson in the editing of the last two volumes of "The Dial." During the first year of this editorship Thoreau was living in Emerson's house, and he read proofs, selected ethnical scriptures, and did other work on the magazine. In the first number edited by Emerson he printed a characteristic paper by Thoreau, that on the "Natural History of Massachusetts." In this for the first time he expressed himself as a lover of Nature, and an intimate student of her daily life. In his diary for September 1, 1842, Hawthorne recorded that Thoreau dined with him on that day, and he put down therein a most interesting and acute description of the poet-naturalist: "He is a keen and delicate observer of nature, — a genuine observer, — which, I suspect, is almost as rare a character as even an original poet; and Nature, in return for his love, seems to adopt him as her especial child, and shows him secrets which few others are allowed to witness.

He is familiar with beast, fish, fowl, and reptile, and has strange stories to tell of adventures and friendly passages with these lower brethren of mortality. Herb and flower, likewise, wherever they grow, whether in garden or wildwood, are his familiar friends. He is also on intimate terms with the clouds, and can tell the portents of storms. It is a characteristic trait, that he has a great regard for the memory of the Indian tribes, whose wild life would have suited him so well; and, strange to say, he seldom walks over a ploughed field without picking up an arrow-point, or other relic of the red man, as if their spirits willed him to be the inheritor of their simple wealth. With all this he has more than a tincture of literature, — a deep and fine taste for poetry, especially for the elder poets, and he is a good writer, — at least he has written a good article, a rambling disquisition on 'Natural History,' in the last 'Dial,' which, he says, was chiefly made up from journals of his own observations. Methinks this article gives a very fair image of his mind and character, — so true, innate, and literal in observation, yet giving the spirit as well as letter of what he sees, even as a lake reflects its wooded banks, showing every leaf, yet giving the wild beauty of the whole scene. Then there are in the article passages of cloudy and dreamy metaphysics, and also passages where his thoughts seem to measure and attune themselves into spontaneous verse, as they rightfully may, since there is real poetry in them. There is a basis of good sense and of moral truth, too, throughout the article, which also is a reflection of his character; for he is not unwise to think and feel, and I find him a healthy and wholesome man to know."

This number, the first of the third volume, contained a short article entitled " Prayers," which was reprinted as Thoreau's in his " Yankee in Canada." In fact, it was prepared by Emerson, and the " Metrical Prayer " only was by Thoreau, and is now printed with his other poems. This article will now be found reprinted as Emerson's in "The Natural History of the Intellect."

To the October number of "The Dial," for 1842, Thoreau contributed eight poems, the titles of which were: "The Black Knight," "The Inward Morning," "Free Love," "The Poet's Delay," "Rumors from an Æolian Harp," "The Moon," "To the Maiden in the East," and "The Summer Rain," all of which were reprinted in "A Week," except "The Black Knight," and "The Moon." "The Black Knight" was first printed in full in "The Boston Commonwealth" for October 30, 1863, then edited by Mr. Frank B. Sanborn, and appears in Henry S. Salt's edition of Thoreau's "Poems of Nature." "The Moon" was for the first time reprinted in Salt's volume.

Two articles in "The Dial" for January, 1843, indicate the aid furnished by Thoreau in editing the periodical. One of these is "The Laws of Menu," selected by Thoreau; and the other, a translation of "The Prometheus Bound" of Æschylus.

The selections from Menu formed the second series of ethnical scriptures published in "The Dial," the first having been made by Emerson, and consisted of selections from what he called the "Veeshnoo Sarma." In this attempt to introduce the Oriental sacred writings to occidental readers, then first undertaken in this country, Thoreau was fully in sympathy with Emerson, as his several volumes abundantly indicate. What Thoreau did was to select, with a judicious hand, from the translation of Sir William Jones, which had appeared fifty years before, but was little known in this country, except to such as Emerson.

The last number of the third volume of "The Dial," that for April, 1843, was almost wholly edited by Thoreau. Emerson was then in New York engaged in lecturing, and he wrote, February 12, giving Thoreau directions as to "The Dial." The first article in this number was an extended review of Alcott's works, written by Charles Lane. It also contained an article on [the pseudo] Anacreon, by Thoreau himself, including translations of eleven poems, reproduced in " A Week." To this number Thoreau contributed three poems. The first of these was " To a Stray Fowl," reprinted by Salt in his collection. Under the title of " Orphics," Thoreau printed in this number two poems ; the one called " Smoke" he included in "Walden," and that called " Haze " in " A Week." The third poem was entitled " Dark Ages," and was included in " A Week." When Emerson wrote from New York to Thoreau about this number of " The Dial" the latter made reply February 15, 1843, writing from Emerson's house : " As a packet is to go in the morning, I will give you a hasty account of ' The Dial.' I called on Mr. Lane this afternoon, and brought away, together with an abundance of good-will, first, a bulky catalogue of books without commentary, — some eight hundred, I think he told me, with an introduction filling one sheet, — ten or a dozen pages, say, though I have only glanced at them ; second, a review — twenty-five or thirty printed pages — of ' Conversations on the Gospels,' ' Record of a School,' and ' Spiritual Culture ' [Alcott's works], with rather copious extracts. However, it is a good subject, and Lane says it gives him satisfaction. I will give it a faithful reading directly. And now I come to the little end of the horn ; for myself, I have brought along the ' Minor Greek Poets,' and will mine there for a scrap or two, at least."

The last reference was to Thoreau's translations of [the pseudo] Anacreon. That in regard to a catalogue of books was to a collection of mystical and idealistic works brought over from England by Alcott and Lane ; and it was printed at the end of this number of " The Dial." It would appear from a letter of Thoreau to Emerson that he revised this catalogue, omitting such books from the list as were not rare.

On the subject of Thoreau's contributions of poetry to
"The Dial" he wrote to Emerson in the letter just quoted:
"Perhaps I have some few scraps in my Journal which you
may choose to print. The translation of the Æschylus I
should like very well to continue anon, if it should be worth
the while. As for poetry, I have not remembered to write
any for some time ; it has quite slipped my mind ; but sometimes I think I hear the mutterings of the thunder. Don't
you remember that last summer we heard a low, tremulous
sound in the woods and over the hills, and thought it was
partridges or rocks, and it proved to be thunder gone down
the river ? But sometimes it was over Wayland way, and
at last burst over our heads. So we 'll not despair by reason
of the drought. You see it takes a good many words to
supply the place of one deed, — a hundred lines to a cobweb,
and but one cable to a man-of-war. 'The Dial' case needs
to be reformed in many particulars."

In a postscript to this letter Thoreau continues the account
of his work in editing the April number of "The Dial." "I
have time to write a few words about 'The Dial,'" he continues. "I have just received the three first signatures,
which do not yet complete Lane's piece. He will place
five hundred copies for sale at Munroe's bookstore. Wheeler
has sent you two full sheets — more about the German
universities — and proper names, which will have to be
printed in alphabetical order for convenience ; what this
one has done, that one is doing, and the other intends to
do. Hammer-Purgstall (Von Hammer) may be one, for
aught I know. However, there are two or three things
in it, as well as names. One of the books of Herodotus
is discovered to be out of place. He says something about
having sent to Lowell, by the last steamer, a budget of
literary news, which he will have communicated to you ere
this. Mr. Alcott has a letter from Heraud [the English
critic and poetaster mentioned in connection with the start-

ing of 'The Dial'], and a book written by him, — 'The
Life of Savonarola,' — which he wishes to have republished
here. Mr. Lane will write a notice of it. Miss Peabody
has sent a 'Notice to the Readers of "The Dial,"' which is
not good."

In another letter, written four days later, Thoreau continued the account of his editorial labors: "I have read Mr.
Lane's review, and can say, speaking for this world and
fallen man, that 'it is good for us.' As they say in geology,
time never fails, there is always enough of it; so I may say,
criticism never fails; but if I go and read elsewhere, I say it
is good, — far better than any notice Mr. Alcott has received, or is likely to receive from another quarter. It is
at any rate 'the other side,' which Boston needs to hear.
I do not send it to you, because time is precious, and because I think you would accept it, after all. After speaking briefly of the fate of Goethe and Carlyle in their own
countries, he says, 'To Emerson in his own circle is but
slowly accorded a worthy response; and Alcott, almost
utterly neglected,' etc. I will strike out what relates to
yourself, and correcting some verbal faults, send the rest
to the printer with Lane's initials. It is frequently easy
to make Mr. Lane more universal and attractive; to write,
for instance, 'universal ends' instead of 'the universal end,'
just as we pull open the petals of a flower with our fingers
where they are confined by its own sweets. Also he had
better not say 'books designed for the nucleus of a Home
University,' until he makes that word 'home' ring solid and
universal too. This is that abominable dialect. He has
just given me a notice of George Bradford's 'Fénelon' for
the Record of the Months, and speaks of extras of the Review and Catalogue, if they are printed, — even a hundred,
or thereabouts. How shall this be arranged?"

In May, 1843, Thoreau went for a time to Staten Island,
to live in the house and teach the children of William

Emerson, the oldest brother of Ralph Waldo Emerson. One of his objects, and, in fact, the chief one, in this change of residence, was to secure an opening into the literary world of New York, that he might thus earn an income. His letters indicate his efforts in this direction, and also why they were not successful. He did not find Staten Island as congenial as Concord, and the home he entered into was not as attractive to him as that he had left. He contributed less to "The Dial" during its last year. He had less time than before for literary work, and perhaps he had less inclination for it. Writing to Emerson almost immediately after reaching Staten Island, May 23, he said: "I should have sent you something for 'The Dial' before, but I have been sick ever since I came here, rather unaccountably, — what with cold, bronchitis, acclimation, etc., still unaccountably. I send you some verses from my journal which will help make a packet. I have not time to correct them, if this goes by Rockwood Hoar." A fortnight later he wrote again: "I have hastily written out something for 'The Dial,' and send it only because you are expecting something, — though something better. It seems idle and Howittish, but it may be of more worth in Concord, where it belongs."

The article thus referred to was probably "A Winter Walk," printed in the October number of "The Dial," and republished in "Excursions." No one would now think of it as in the style of William Howitt, the English descriptive writer, or in that of his wife, Mary Howitt. To the July number Thoreau was not a contributor, and of it he wrote to Emerson: "I think this is a noble number of 'The Dial.' It perspires thought and feeling. I can speak of it now a little like a foreigner. Be assured that it is not written in vain, — it is not for me. I hear its prose and its verse. They provoke and inspire me, and they have my sympathy. I hear the sober and the earnest, the sad and the cheery

voices of my friends, and to me it is a long letter of encouragement and reproof; and no doubt so it is to many another
in the land. So don't give up the ship. Methinks the
verse is hardly enough better than the prose. I give my
vote for the 'Notes from the Journal of a Scholar' [by
Charles Chauncy Emerson], and wonder you don't print
them faster. I want, too, to read the rest of 'The Poet and
the Painter' [by Ellery Channing]. Miss Fuller's is a
noble piece ['The Great Lawsuit,' first form of 'Woman in
the Nineteenth Century,' her best book], — rich extem-
pore writing, talking with pen in hand. It is too good not
to be better, even. In writing, conversation should be
folded many times thick. It is the height of art that, on
the first perusal, plain common-sense should appear; on the
second, severe truth; and on a third, beauty; and, having
these warrants for its depth and reality, we may then enjoy
the beauty for evermore. The sea-piece is of the best that
is going, if not the best that is staying [Hunt's account of
a voyage to Jamaica]. You have spoken a good word for
Carlyle [review of 'French Revolution,' in article entitled
'Past and Present']. As for the 'Winter's Walk,' I should
be glad to have it printed in 'The Dial,' if you think it
good enough, and will criticise it; otherwise send it to me,
and I will dispose of it." Emerson also thought well of
this number of "The Dial," for he wrote to Thoreau: "Our
'Dial' thrives well enough in these weeks. I print W. E.
Channing's Letters ['The Youth of the Poet and the
Painter'], or the first ones, but he does not care to have
them named as his for a while. They are very agreeable
reading, and their wisdom lightened by a vivacity very
rare in 'The Dial.' [S. G.] Ward, too, has sent me some
sheets on architecture, whose good sense is eminent. I have
a valuable manuscript — a sea voyage — from a new hand,
which is all clear good sense, and I may make some of Mr.
Lane's graver sheets give way for this honest story [Hunt's

voyage to Jamaica] ; otherwise I shall print it in October. I have transferred the publishing of ' The Dial ' to James Munroe & Co." In a postscript, written five days later, he added : " Whilst my letter has lain on the table waiting for a traveller, your letter and parcel have safely arrived. I may not have place now for the ' Winter's Walk ' in the July ' Dial,' which is just making up its last sheets, and somehow I must end it to-morrow, when I go to Boston. I shall, then, keep it for October, subject, however, to your order, if you find a better disposition for it."

Writing of " A Winter Walk " to Thoreau, on September 8, 1843, Emerson said : " I mean to send the 'Winter's Walk ' to the printer to-morrow for ' The Dial.' I had some hesitation about it, notwithstanding its faithful observation and its fine sketches of the pickerel fisher and of the woodchopper, on account of the *mannerism,* an old charge of mine, — as if, by attention, one could get the trick of the rhetoric ; for example, to call a cold place sultry, a solitude public, a wilderness *domestic* (a favorite word), and in the woods to insult our cities, armies, etc. By pretty free omissions, however, I have removed my principal objections. I ought to say that Ellery Channing admired the piece loudly and long, and only stipulated for the omission of Douglas and one copy of verses on the Smoke. For the rest, we go on with ' The Youth of the Poet and Painter ' and the extracts from the ' Jamaica Voyage,' and Lane has sent me ' A Day with the Shakers.' Poetry have I very little. Have you no Greek translations ready for me ? "

Concerning Emerson's excisions from " A Winter Walk," Thoreau wrote him on September 14: " I doubt if you have made more corrections in my manuscript than I should have done ere this, though they may be better ; but I am glad you have taken any pains with it. I have not prepared any translations for ' The Dial,' supposing there would be no room, though it is the only place for them."

Emerson did cut out two or more pages from " A Winter Walk," and made many other revisions. The excised pages are now in the possession of Frank B. Sanborn, who has included some of them in his " Personality of Thoreau." The poem cut off from the end of the essay was as follows:

> " Pray to what earth does this sweet cold belong,
> Which asks no duties and no conscience?
> The moon goes up by leaps her cheerful path,
> In some far summer stratum of the sky,
> While stars with their cold shine bedot her way.
> The fields gleam mildly back upon the sky,
> And far and near upon the leafless shrubs
> The snow dust still emits a silvery light.

> " Under the hedge, where drift-banks are their screen,
> The titmice now pursue their downy dreams,
> As often in the sweltering summer nights
> The bee doth drop asleep in the flower-cup,
> When evening overtakes him with his load.

> " By the brooksides, in the still genial night,
> The more adventurous wanderer may hear
> The crystals shoot and form, and Winter slow
> Increase his rule by gentlest summer means."

In connection with these verses Thoreau wrote the following prose paragraph, also cut out by Emerson: " From our comfortable pillows we lend our warm sympathy to the Siberian traveller, on whose morning route the sun is rising, and in imagination frequent the encampment of the lonely fur-trader on Lake Winnipeg; and climb the Ural or the Jura, or range the Andes and the Rocky mountains, or traverse the shaggy solitudes of the glaciers, — in our dreams hugging the furs about us. Or perhaps we have visions of Greece and Italy, the Ægean Sea and the Sicilian coast; or anticipate the coming in of spring like a pomp through the gate of a city."

Another poem, written about 1841, and sent by Thoreau to " The Dial," was rejected, and is for the first time printed by Mr. Sanborn in his delightful book, which is one of the best interpretations of Thoreau's life and character yet given to the public :

OUR COUNTRY.

It is a noble country where we dwell,
Fit for a stalwart race to summer in ;
From Madawaska to Red River raft,
From Florid keys to the Missouri forks,
See what unwearied and copious streams
Come tumbling to the east and southern shore,
To find a man stand on their lowland banks :
Behold the innumerous rivers and the licks
Where he may drink to quench his summer's thirst,
And the broad corn and rice fields yonder, where
His hands may gather for his winter's store.

See the fair reaches of the northern lakes
To cool his summer with their inland breeze,
And the long slumbering Appalachian range
Offering its slopes to his unwearied knees !
See what a long-lipped sea doth clip the shores,
And noble strands where navies may find port ;
See Boston, Baltimore, and New York stand
Fair in the sunshine on the eastern sea,
And yonder too the fair green prairie.

See the red race with sullen step retreat,
Emptying its graves, striking the wigwam tent,
And where the rude camps of its brethren stand
Dotting the distant green, their herds around ;
In serried ranks, and with a distant clang,
Their fowls fly o'er, bound to the northern lakes,
Whose plashing waves invite their webbéd feet.

Such the fair reach and prospect of the land.
The journeying summer creeps from south to north
With wearied feet, resting in many a vale ;
Its length doth tire the seasons to o'ercome,
Its widening breadth doth make the sea-breeze pause
And spend its breath against the mountain's side :
Still serene Summer paints the southern fields,
While the stern Winter reigns on northern hills.

Look nearer, — know the lineaments of each face, —
Learn the far-travelled race, and find here met
The so long gathering congress of the world !
The Afric race brought here to curse its fate,
Erin to bless, — the patient German too,
Th' industrious Swiss, the fickle, sanguine Gaul,
And manly Saxon, leading all the rest ;
All things invite this earth's inhabitants
To rear their lives to an unheard-of height,
And meet the expectation of the land;
To give at length the restless race of man
A pause in the long westering caravan.

It is not difficult to understand why Emerson, with his fastidious taste, should have thought it best not to publish the poems and the paragraph just presented. They are not equal to Thoreau's best poetical work, and they do not justify our estimate of his genius, however gladly we read them, now that everything from his pen has gained worth for us.

In a letter written to Emerson, October 17, Thoreau speaks of meeting in New York William Tappan, a contributor to "The Dial": "I should have liked to hear more news from his lips, though he had left me a letter and ' The Dial,' which is a sort of circular letter itself. I find Channing's letters ['The Youth of the Poet and the Painter'] full of life, and I enjoy their wit keenly. Lane writes straight and solid on [Social Tendencies], like a guideboard, but I find I put off the social tendencies to a future day, which may never come. He is always Shaker fare, quite as luxurious as his principles will allow. [Lane lived with the Harvard Shakers, near by, after Fruitlands was abandoned.] I see that I was very blind to send you my manuscript ['A Winter Walk'] in such a state ; but I have a good second sight, at least. I could still shake it in the wind to some advantage, if it would hold together. There are some sad mistakes in the printing. It is a little unfortunate that the 'Ethnical Scriptures' [the Chinese 'Kings,' selected by Thoreau] should hold out so well, though it does really hold out. The Bible ought not to be very large. Is it not singular that, while the religious world is gradually picking to pieces its old testaments, here are some coming slowly after, on the seashore, picking up the durable relics of perhaps older books, and putting them together again ?

"Your 'Letter to Contributors' is excellent, and hits the nail on the head. It will taste sour to their palates at first, no doubt, but it will bear a sweet fruit at last. I like the poetry, especially the Autumn verses [by Ellery Channing]. They ring true. Though I am quite weather-beaten with poetry, having weathered so many epics of late. The 'Sweep Ho!' [by Mrs. Ellen Hooper] sounds well this way. But I have a great deal of fault to find with your ' Ode to Beauty.' The tune is altogether unworthy of the thought. You slope too quickly to the rhyme, as if that trick had better be performed as soon as possible, or as if you stood over the line with a hatchet, and chopped off the verses as they came out, some short and some long. But give us a long reel, and we'll cut it up to suit ourselves. It sounds like parody. 'Thee knew I of old,' 'Remediless thirst,' are some of these stereotyped lines. I am frequently reminded, I believe, of Jane Taylor's ' Philosopher's Scales,' and how the world —

> ' Flew out with a bounce,'

which —

> 'Yerked the philosopher out of his cell ;'

or else of —

> ' From the climes of the sun all war-worn and weary.'

I had rather have the thought come ushered with a flourish of oaths and curses. Yet I love your poetry as I do little else that is near and recent, especially when you get fairly round the end of the line, and are not thrown back upon the rocks. To read the lecture on 'The Comic' [by Emerson] is as good as to be in our town meeting or Lyceum once more."

These criticisms on Emerson's poem show that Thoreau could hit hard as a critic when he chose to do so ; and it may be that he was provoked thereto by the severity with which his own work had been handled by Margaret Fuller and Emerson. That his criticisms were not without effect may be seen in at least one change made by Emerson in his "Ode to Beauty." The lines in "The Dial" referred to by Thoreau were :

> "Love drinks at thy banquet
> Remediless thirst,"

which were greatly improved when they were changed to

> "Love drinks at thy fountain
> False waters of thirst."

To the number of "The Dial" for January, 1844, Thoreau contributed extracts from a lecture on Homer, Ossian, and Chaucer he had delivered before the Concord Lyceum, November 29, 1843, which has not been reprinted. He also selected, probably, "The Preaching of Buddha," in the series of "Ethnical Scriptures." To the last number he furnished a notice of the fearless anti-slavery labors of a New Hampshire editor, Nathaniel P. Rogers, whose "Herald of Freedom" was brilliantly edited. This paper was appended to "A Yankee in Canada," but in the Riverside edition it was given a place in the "Miscellanies." To these concluding numbers of "The Dial" Thoreau contributed two series of translations of Pindar, which have also been added to the "Miscellanies" in the Riverside edition. The incentive to the translation of Pindar seems to have come from Charles Newcomb, one of the minor contributors to "The Dial." Writing to Thoreau, July 20, Emerson said : "I saw Charles Newcomb the other day at Brook Farm, and he expressed his satisfaction in your translations, and said that he had been minded to write you and ask of you to translate in like manner — Pindar. I advised him by all means to do so. But he seemed to think he had discharged his conscience. But it was a very good request. It would be a fine thing to be done, since Pindar has no adequate translation, — no English equal to his fame. Do look at the book with that in your mind, while Charles is mending his pen."

It appears that Thoreau's first essay that has in any form appeared in print was that entitled "The Service: Qualities of the Recruit." It was sent to Margaret Fuller for "The Dial," but she rejected it in a letter dated December 1, 1841. "I am to blame," she writes, "for so long detaining your manuscript. But my thoughts have been so engaged that I have not found a suitable hour to re-read it as I wished, till last night. The second reading only confirms my impression from the first. The essay is rich in thoughts, and I should be pained not to meet it again. But then, the thoughts seem to me so out of their natural order that I cannot read it through without pain. I never once feel myself in a stream of thought, but seem to hear the grating of tools on the mosaic. It is true, as Mr. Emerson says, that essays not to be compared with this have found their way into 'The Dial.' But then, these are more unassuming in their tone, and have an air of quiet good-breeding, which induces us to permit their presence. Yours is so rugged that it ought to be commanding."

Brief selections from "The Service" were read at the Concord School of Philosophy, in 1882, by Mr. Frank B. Sanborn. These were printed in the "Concord Lectures in Philosophy" published by Moses King of Cambridge, and in the "Miscellanies" of the Riverside edition of Thoreau's works. This essay has been edited from Thoreau's manuscript by Mr. Sanborn, and published in Boston by Charles

E. Goodspeed, who has also published Mr. Sanborn's little book on "The Personality of Thoreau."

His initiative into literature was afforded Thoreau by "The Dial." It gave him a public, and it gave him confidence in himself. He carefully utilized much of what he printed therein in the preparation of his first books, and most of the rest has been printed in the volumes edited by his friends. In these earliest productions of his pen the aboriginal Thoreau appeared, however meekly he accepted the criticisms of his editorial friends.

Thoreau became an inmate of Emerson's house in April, 1841, and he continued there until the spring of 1843, when he went to Staten Island, where he wrote his poem called "The Departure." About November, 1843, Thoreau returned to Concord, and lived with his father, mother, and two sisters, until he built his hut on the shore of Walden pond, in March, 1845. In the autumn of 1847 Emerson went to England to lecture, and Thoreau left his hut to become an inmate again of Emerson's house, and to care for its outward concerns in the owner's absence. During the period included in those dates Thoreau was perfecting himself as an author, and the methods he pursued may be indicated in his own words, some of which are not generally known to the public.

"For the last five years," Thoreau wrote to Horace Greeley from Concord, May 19, 1848, "I have supported myself solely by the labor of my hands. I have not received one cent from any other source, and this has cost me so little time, say a month in the spring and another in the autumn, doing the coarsest work of all kinds, that I have probably enjoyed more leisure for literary pursuits than any contemporary. For more than two years past I have lived alone in the woods, in a good plastered and shingled house entirely of my own building, earning only what I wanted and sticking to my proper work. The fact is man need not live by the sweat of his brow — unless he sweats easier than I do — he needs so little. For two years and two months all my expenses have amounted to but 27 cents a week, and I have fared gloriously in all respects. If a man must have money — and he needs but the smallest amount, the true and independent way to earn it is by day labor with his hands at a dollar a day — I have tried many ways and can speak from experience. Scholars are apt to think themselves privileged to complain as if their lot was a peculiarly hard one. How much have we heard about the attainment of knowledge under difficulties, of poets starving in garrets — depending on the patronage of the wealthy — and finally dying mad. It is time men sang another song. There is no reason why the scholar who professes to be a little wiser than the mass of men, should not do his work in the ditch occasionally, and by means of his superior wisdom make much less suffice for him. A wise man will not be unfortunate. How then would you know but he was a fool?"

Another most interesting glimpse into the way in which Thoreau regarded himself and his own special work is afforded by the Memorials of the 1837 Class of Harvard University. Writing to the class secretary, in 1847, in answer to a circular asking for information about the lives of the class members during the first decade of their professional life, Thoreau gave this highly interesting and characteristic account of himself: "Am not married. I don't know whether mine is a profession, or a trade, or what not. It is not yet learned, in every instance has been practised before being studied. The mercantile part of it was begun by myself alone. It is not one, but legion. I will give you some of the monster's heads. I am a schoolmaster, a private tutor, a sawyer, a gardener, a farmer, a painter (I mean a house-painter), a carpenter, a mason, a day-laborer, a pencil-maker, a glass-paper-maker, a writer, and sometimes a poetaster. If you will act the part of Iolas, and apply a hot iron to any of these heads, I shall be greatly obliged to you. My present employment is to answer such orders as may be expected from so general an advertisement as the above. That is, if I see fit, which is not always the case, for I have found out a way to live without what is commonly called employment, or industry, attractive or otherwise. Indeed, my steadiest employment, if such it can be called, is to keep myself on the top of my condition, and ready for whatever may turn up in heaven or on earth. The last two or three years I have lived in Concord woods, alone, something more than a mile from any neighbor, in a house built entirely by myself. P. S. I beg that the class will not consider me an object of charity, and if any of them are in want of any pecuniary assistance, and will make known their case to me, I will engage to give them some advice of more worth than money." In another letter to the class secretary he indicated his early and passionate love of Nature, and that this interfered with his college studies : " Though bodily I have been a member of Harvard University, heart and soul I have been far away among the scenes of my boyhood. Those hours that should have been devoted to study have been spent in scouring the woods and exploring the lakes and streams of my native village. Immured within the dark but classic walls of a Stoughton or a Hollis, my spirit yearned for the sympathy of my old and almost forgotten friend, Nature."

His period of apprenticeship to Nature began with Thoreau at about the time " The Dial " came to its end, and it was one of the greatest importance to him. In his book about his Walden life Thoreau says that in March, 1845, he borrowed an axe and went into the woods to build him a house. This axe was procured from Emerson, and Thoreau says he returned it sharper than when he borrowed it. He says that he was assisted in building his house by some of his acquaintances, "rather to improve so good an occasion for neighborliness than from any necessity." These acquaintances, who were really all intimate friends, were Emerson, Alcott, Ellery Channing, Burrill and George William Curtis, Edmund Hosmer, and his sons John, Edmund, and Andrew. He wished the help of the young men, Thoreau said, because they had more strength than the older ones who aided him, and that no man was ever more honored in the character of his raisers than he.

What would Thoreau have been without transcendentalism? It afforded him entrance to the secrets of Nature and it made him a true interpreter of the outward world. It has been complained that he was not a scientific observer, that his knowledge was limited, and his methods imperfect. It is true that he was a poet and not a scientist, but it is that very fact which made him in large degree the incarnate voice of Nature. Had he been a keener scientific observer he would have been less a poet, and his literary skill would have been deficient. The more scientific interpreters of the outward world who have followed him have shown little of his genius, and they have lost in originality as they have gained in accuracy. Thoreau was not a genius because he was unscientific; but he saw Nature as a whole with wonderful insight, and with a skill no mere plodding can equal. Every year since his death has brought him added fame; for his originality, his charm of utterance, and his large spiritual insight, endear him to many, who find in his brave words that which makes Nature closest friend and companion.

IX

ELIZABETH P. PEABODY

NOT less as a contributor to "The Dial" than as one of its publishers does Elizabeth Palmer Peabody deserve recognition. To the second number of the second volume she contributed an article entitled "A Glimpse of Christ's Idea of Society." This paper was first sent as a letter to Harriet Martineau, at the request of George Ripley. It was followed in the third number by an account of the "Plan of the West Roxbury Community." These articles were the result of her intimate acquaintance with Dr. Channing, as well as with George Ripley. In her "Reminiscences of Dr. Channing" she showed how fully he was in sympathy with Ripley in his Brook Farm experiment. She said that Channing "agreed with Ripley in the important proposition that it was entirely impossible to live under our civilization without being an involuntary party to great social wrong all the time. Division of labor, he said, was good for the acquisition of national wealth, but sacrificed the individuals composing the nation. He therefore looked upon Ripley's plans with interest and favor, although he had a thousand doubts about its immediate success. The year before, when Jonathan Phillips [one of the most active supporters of Dr. Channing in his charity and church work] was living at the Tremont House, there had been a meeting in his parlor, playfully named the Club of Jacobins, which was frequented by George Ripley, John S. Dwight, Theodore Parker, and other critics of the times, who talked of social reforms; and these meetings greatly interested Dr. Channing. . . . He was most interested in the enterprise as an illustration of the practicability of uniting manual labor with intellectual pursuits. He wanted our agricultural population to see that the land could get cultivated, and that in the best manner, while neither themselves nor their children were made beasts of burden; that leisure could be redeemed for intellectual pursuits and the arts that adorn life ; and through a levelling-up process, the distinction of classes disappear by the universalizing of good manners."

Miss Peabody's 'intimate association with Dr. Channing at this period brought her into sympathy with Mr. Ripley and his efforts for the reformation of society. She did not become a member of the Brook Farm community, probably restrained therefrom because Dr. Channing could not give it his full sympathy, and because she was greatly influenced by Emerson's individualism, as opposed to the idea of association. However, her communications to " The Dial " indicate the fulness of her appreciation of the effort being made by Ripley and his associates. The restraining influences that kept her from connecting herself with Brook Farm may be seen in the other paper she contributed to " The Dial," and which appeared in the last number under the title " Fourierism." It was written at the time when Brook Farm was introducing the theories of Fourier. The article is a general report of the substance of what was said concerning the teachings of Fourier at a convention held in Boston during the last days of 1843 and the first of 1844. At that time members of the several communities then existing in New England and New York met to discuss the problems of association, with the result that Fourierism was adopted at Brook Farm, owing to the zealous efforts of Albert Brisbane and William Henry Channing. Miss Peabody did not accept the teachings of Fourier without qualification, and she expressed doubts as to their results when put into practice at Brook Farm. Her articles on " Christ's Idea of Society " and on " Fourierism " were reprinted in her

"Last Evening with Allston, and Other Papers," published in 1886.

Elizabeth Palmer Peabody was born in Billerica, Mass., May 16, 1804, the daughter of Nathaniel Peabody, a physician for many years in Salem and Boston. Her mother was a very capable and efficient teacher, one of the earliest and most successful of the women who took up that profession. They were teaching in Andover, Mass., he as the principal of the boys' school there, and she of that for girls, when they became acquainted, and were soon after married. They removed to Billerica, a few miles distant, in order that he might study medicine with a prominent physician there; and she opened a boarding-school with thirty pupils. Here Elizabeth was born; but in 1805 the family removed to Cambridge for one year, in order that Mr. Peabody might complete his medical education. Then they settled in Lynn, he as a physician, and she to her work as a teacher, being for some time at the head of an academy. In 1808 they removed to Salem, which was their home for many years.

Mrs. Peabody was a highly educated woman for her day, and she was a teacher for eighteen years. She was thoughtful, original, and capable, inventing her own methods, and using them with rare skill. She was influenced by the ideas of women then dominant, and by the social theory that they must be retiring and subordinate; but she had a high ideal for women and of their mission as teachers. She thought that women should not be taught in too robust and independent a manner, but she was remarkably broad-minded for her time. Writing of her own methods as a teacher, Miss Peabody said that " they were implicitly suggested by my mother, who followed her motherly instinct with her own children. She always seemed to me an entirely different and generally opposite influence to that of all others with whom I came in contact. My mother's idea of education was predominantly moral — to fill my mind with images of kind, heroic, and thoroughly high-principled people, which her fine instinct picked out of society around us, as well as from history and literature. Every kind of hollow pretension was her supreme abhorrence; all moral affectation and religious cant she saw through; and the nervous weakness of self-indulgent fine ladies she thoroughly despised. But she was not censorious of individuals nor wanting in tenderness, and referred their faults so invariably to bad education or no education that when I entered on this vocation myself — a vocation for which she educated me, considering it the highest and the proper activity of every American woman who loved her country — moral education became to my mind the essence of all education, and I never thought of any intellectual acquisition nor of any artistic power except as subservient to moral and social ends."

It was the aim of Mrs. Peabody to make her pupils familiar with history as affording motives for moral action, and with the best literature as giving the mind intellectual and spiritual incentives. Her range of subjects was somewhat narrow, but her method was novel, and it was effective. It made her pupils familiar with all the great English writers, and it gave them the capacity of enjoying and appreciating them. Such was the training received by Elizabeth Peabody, and it admirably fitted her for her work as teacher, lecturer, and author. Her father taught her Latin in an old-fashioned but effective manner; and at a later time she was instructed in German and French by those native to these languages. Her education was quite unusually thorough and wide of range for the early part of the nineteenth century.

At the age of sixteen Elizabeth Peabody became a teacher. In 1820 the family moved to Lancaster, Mass., and there she taught for two years, some of her pupils of both sexes being older than herself. The medical practice of her father proving not to be what it had been represented, he removed to Boston. Elizabeth opened a school in Mount Vernon street, and after two years she went to Gardiner, Maine, where she was the tutor in a wealthy family of English Unitarians. In 1825 she took up the work of teaching in Brookline, and was in intimate intercourse with Dr. Channing, acting as his amanuensis, reading to him from French and German books, and making record of his conversations and his sermons, which she afterwards published in her "Reminiscences." In 1826 Dr. Channing put his daughter Mary under Miss Peabody's care in a school gathered for her by Eliza Lee Cabot, who became the wife of Dr. Charles Follen, the German exile and scholar, and the intimate friend of Channing. In this school she continued for seven years, and it was highly successful. Interest in the methods pursued by Amos Bronson Alcott in his famous Temple School led Miss Peabody to volunteer her services as his assistant on the opening of the school in September, 1834. In his diary Alcott wrote of her as one " whose reputation, both as regards original and acquired ability, is high, — she unites intellectual and practical qualities of no common order." The school was placed in her charge in the afternoons, when she taught Latin and geography ; and she also recorded Mr. Alcott's conversations with his pupils in the mornings. In June, 1835, was published the first volume of these conversations under the title of " Record of a School." Early in 1837 appeared two volumes of " Conversations with Children on the Gospels," from the reports of Miss Peabody, though a few of the conversations were recorded by her sister, Sophia Peabody, who became the wife of Hawthorne. The result of the publication of these volumes was the closing of the Temple School, most of the pupils being withdrawn because of the criticisms to which it was subjected in the newspapers and elsewhere. In later years, the " Record of a School " was twice reprinted, on each occasion receiving revision in order to give it fidelity to Miss Peabody's growing educational theories.

During these years of teaching Miss Peabody was at work as an author, chiefly along educational lines. She published an " Introduction to Grammar," " First Steps to History," " Key to the History of the Hebrews," " Keys to Grecian History," and other works, mostly text-books. She also translated De Gérando's " Visitor to the Poor." After leaving the Temple School she went to live in Salem with her parents, but she continued her educational work with adults, already begun in Boston. This consisted of conversations with women on historical and educational subjects, the first course being held in Boston in 1833, and another in 1836. Two other courses were given, in 1844 and 1845. For about twenty years she devoted much of her time to this work of teaching women history and literature by means of what she called " conferences," which were partly devoted to lectures by her, partly to the reading of essays by members of the class, and partly to conversation on the topic of the day. As she began these conferences in 1833, she preceded Margaret Fuller in the holding of conversations, who did not begin hers until November, 1839, and then under Miss Peabody's auspices. As the pioneer in this kind of educational work, which has led up to the women's clubs of the present day, it is interesting to have Miss Peabody's own account of her methods, which she gave in an article prepared for " Barnard's Journal of Education."

" My classes met me twice a week, and took the shape of Historical Conferences. For instance, I will describe one of the several I had in three different cities. The term was six months, admitting of fifty sessions. I proposed to take up ancient history before the eighth century, when there was no pretence anywhere of a historical record of events, and little biography of persons except in the old Hebrew Scriptures, but history was to be guessed out by researches among ancient monuments. The text-books I used were Heeren's 'Researches in Ancient India, Persia, Babylon, Egypt, Ethiopia, Phœnicia, and Ancient Greece;' Layard's 'Nineveh,' Landseer's 'Cylinders of Babylon,' Karl Otfried Müller's 'History of the Dorians' and his work on the 'Etruscans.' There were enough ladies in the class for each to take a separate country, concerning which she read as much as she could at home between the sessions. We met at ten o'clock, and each lady put into my hands a few questions that she had written to guide me in bringing out from her what proved a lecture to the rest, who in turn all lectured to her, and thus was brought before us all that was going on in these several civilizations, more or less isolated from each other. My part was to put in the Hebrew life at the time, and help to compare these contemporaneous developments of humanity so far as the antiquities accessible serve to elucidate it. The plan proved a great success, and our sessions were sometimes prolonged for four hours, so interesting were the conversations. The ladies made their recitations in answer to the questions either viva voce or by abstracts, or read extracts from books. Müller's 'Etruscans' being in German, the accomplished lady who took it made a free translation of the whole of it. The next year another conference took up the eight centuries immediately preceding Christ. Our text-books were Herodotus, Thucydides, Xenophon, Livy, and Plutarch. We proceeded contemporaneously with the divisions of Sardanapalus's empire, the Israelites and Jews, Persia, Greece, and Rome, sometimes taking a century, sometimes half or quarter of a century, sometimes a decade, and after the recitation or abstract, to aid which I wrote and printed my 'Keys to Grecian History,' that consist only of questions, we would converse; and I read to them K. O. Müller's 'History of Greek Literature,' some of August Schlegel's lectures on the 'Greek theatre,' Mitchell's 'Introduction to Aristophanes,' Xenophon's 'Memorabilia of Socrates,' and Plato's 'Eutyphron,' 'Apology of Socrates,' 'Crito' and 'Phædo;' and I think we took some extra sessions to read translations of the Greek tragedies. There were some of the Hebrew students, brothers and friends of my scholars, who came to me sub rosa while this conference was going on, and asked my advice as to their historical reading, who followed out this course and read the tragedies, and I advised them to read the Greek historians and Livy in the originals. There was at that time no professor of history in any college in the United States."

The conferences of 1844 were devoted to the eighteenth century, and to the causes that led to the French Revolution. So late as 1866 Miss Peabody returned to this work of historical instruction, though more distinctly in the form of lectures. In that year she read a historical paper in the parlor of Mrs. Josiah Quincy, and those present were so much interested by it that they besought her to give them a course of historical lectures, which resulted in her preparing twenty lectures on the great civilizations of antiquity. She said of these lectures that they were very imperfect as literary productions, but they deeply interested those who heard them, and they were frequently repeated in the parlors of her friends, in several cities.

In 1839 Miss Peabody again removed to Boston, this time to open a book-store at 13 West Street, then at the south end of the city. She kept periodicals for sale, as well as foreign books, and, at the suggestion and with the assistance of Washington Allston, painter's materials. This book-store was the first one in Boston where foreign books, especially French and German, were kept on sale and could be ordered. One side of it was occupied by her father, who sold homeopathic medicines, then as much an innovation as the reading of foreign books. Miss Peabody was not only a book-seller, but she was also a publisher. The first book she issued from the press was Dr. Channing's work on "Emancipation," which he put into her hands in order to encourage her in this enterprise. Although he gave her the copyright, yet she so far relinquished it as to permit the various anti-slavery societies throughout the country to bring out cheap editions, with the result that she did not sell the edition of one thousand copies she had printed. She brought out other books, but the competition of the other book-sellers made it impossible for her to succeed. Concerning this experience she wrote: "About 1840 I came to Boston and opened the business of importing and publishing foreign books, a thing not then attempted by any one. I had also a foreign library of new French and German books; and then I came into contact with the world as never before. The Ripleys were starting Brook Farm, and they were friends of ours. Theodore Parker was beginning his career, and all these things were discussed in my book-store by Boston lawyers and Cambridge professors. Those were very living years for me. Being so much occupied as I was at this time I was obliged to deny myself to my friends, except on Wednesday evenings; and I may be said to have set the fashion in Boston of having regular reception evenings. The book-publishers combined against me, and though my friend Dr. Channing gave me his 'Emancipation,' and Hawthorne his 'Grandfather's Chair,' yet I could not fight them all successfully, and finally relinquished business."

For several years Miss Peabody's book-store was a notable centre of intellectual and reformatory interest. There every question of the day was discussed, and there all the new books were subjected to faithful criticism. Brook Farm was carefully considered there for many months before it became a fact, and it was talked over by Ripley, Parker, Brownson, Dwight, Warren Burton, Samuel Robbins, Adin Ballou, and others, in that friendly place of meeting. These men agreed

Elizabeth P. Peabody

in being discontented with society as it then existed, and they were united in wishing for a humaner and juster form of social organization. In this little book-store they debated all features of the problems thus presented, stating their differences with charity and good-will, and yet inciting each other to make the effort to secure a better form of social existence. In the same place all phases of theological opinion found expression, especially those that were in any way individualistic or in harmony with the social reforms of the day. The come-outers of all kinds were sure to find each other in this place, and to find there fit audience for their theories. It is related of W. H. Channing, by his biographer, that he had come, in the winter of 1841–42, to doubt in regard to all forms of church organization. He went into Miss Peabody's book-store, and a discussion arose on the miracles, during which he said that Jesus mistook the impulse of beneficence for the power to set aside natural laws. To this some one present, perhaps Miss Peabody herself, replied that such a theory made Christ insane, denied free-will, and made God incapable of spiritual activity. Channing did not reply, but went away, secluded himself for some weeks, and then came forth a most pronounced Christian believer. On the next Sunday he gave a most eloquent vindication of his new and radiant faith. Col. T. W. Higginson says the Brook Farm people were often to be met in Miss Peabody's " atom of a shop." " There I made acquaintance," he continues, " with Cousin and Jouffroy, with Constant's ' De la Religion' and Leroux' 'De l'Humanité,' the relics of the French eclecticism, then beginning to fade, but still taught in colleges. There, too, were Schubert's ' Geschichte der Seele' and many of the German balladists, who were beginning to enthrall me. There was Miss Peabody herself, desultory, dreamy, but insatiable in her love for knowledge and for helping others to it. James Freeman Clarke said of her that she was always engaged in supplying some want

149

that had first to be created; it might be Dr. Kraitsir's lectures on language, or General Bem's historical chart. She always preached the need, but never accomplished the supply until she advocated the Kindergarten; there she caught up with her mission and came to identify herself with its history."

The period from 1850 to 1860 Miss Peabody devoted to the advancement of the study of history in the schools of the country. In connection therewith she published several historical works, a number of them text-books. As the result of her acquaintance with several natives of Poland, exiled from that country because of their love of liberty, she published, in 1850, her book on "The Crimes of the House of Austria against Mankind," into which she compressed with burning indignation a complete record of autocratic despotism on the part of the royal family of Austria. Among her Polish friends was one by the name of Podbielski, who brought to this country a system of historical charts, which had been invented and used in his country. It was introduced into France, in 1832–40, by General Bem, who had successfully given it a place in the schools of that country. Miss Peabody revised and extended this chart, explained it to Longfellow, George B. Emerson, Dr. Barnas Sears, and others. She published this work, as revised by her, in New York, in 1852, as "Bem's Polish-American System of Chronology." It afforded a mnemonic aid to memory, as well as giving a systematic outline of the chief events of history. In 1856 she published a history of the United States for schools arranged on this plan. Rowland G. Hazard's "Essay on Language, and other Papers," was edited and published by her in 1857. Hazard was a native and a resident of Rhode Island, who had become an intimate friend of Dr. Channing by means of their common philosophical studies. Through Channing Miss Peabody became acquainted with him, with the result that she brought his volume to the

attention of the public. In 1859 she published a translation of De Gérando's "Self Education," and a biographical
sketch of William Wesselhoeft, one of the earliest Boston
homeopathic physicians.

Miss Peabody was always an enthusiast, and she undertook nothing to which she did not give the most devoted
service. Her enthusiasm for Bem's chronological system
was great and lasting, as were all her other educational
affections. In 1871 Count Zaba brought to this country
a revised form of it, or one of similar import, and it made
a great impression in Boston, Cambridge, Chicago, Canada,
and elsewhere. "If I were twenty-five years younger," she
wrote of this method of teaching history, "I would renew
the effort I made in 1850 and the years after, to univer-
salize this method by carrying it over the State myself, which
was interrupted by the Civil War when it was in the full
tide of successful experiment, and still hope, before I die,
to set it a-going by enlisting some one as enthusiastic and
persevering as myself to do it." This enthusiastic coad-
jutor did not appear, and Bem's "System of Chronology" is
now as dead and forgotten as possible, her zeal for it not
serving to keep it before the public.

Miss Peabody was a born teacher, and with a real genius
for imparting instruction. From her childhood to extreme
old age she was constantly engaged in this profession, often
changing her methods of activity, but never getting away
for any length of time from the one passion of her life, that
of educating mankind. Whatever was the immediate subject of her interest her enthusiasm for it was of the most
intense nature, and she could not think or talk of anything
else. Emerson once said of her enthusiasms, "Miss Peabody
always keeps a whole stud of Phœnixes on hand." Her next
enthusiasm was for the Kindergarten, and it proved to be
fortunate and successful. It was the one passion of her life
that the public came to approve and to accept. Her whole

previous career as a teacher had prepared her for this work, and she took it up in a true apostolic spirit, believing it the one means by which mankind was to be redeemed from its social, intellectual, and spiritual defects.

It may be said of Miss Peabody that she followed as a teacher the spirit and intent of transcendentalism. She attempted to draw out from her pupils that which was in them, not to give them something from without, but to open their own inward lives, to produce in them the results of self-development. "My secret is," she wrote, "that I never undertake to manage my pupils. I have no power of commanding. I never do command children, but am very respectful and courteous to them, and throw myself on their mercy, as it were, by telling them of the obligation I am under to their parents and to God to help them educate themselves. I take great pains not to reprove or exhort them before each other, but only in tête-à-tête or by writing a note to them. The relation has no antagonism in it, but is altogether sympathetic. Another principle of my discipline was to avoid exciting a spirit of rivalry, and to have no emulation. I had no marks of merit, no going up or down in classes, and required the whole recitation from each scholar, which at first would seem the longest way, but proved in the end the shortest, because it was so absolutely thorough, and it almost precluded the necessity of repetition and review. In short, I lived with my scholars as Froebel says we should always do with our children. They were always writing to me as to a confessor, in after life, to get my moral and spiritual advice." This was so near to the idea and method of Froebel that she most readily took up his theory when she came to know of it. It was first brought to her attention by the wife of Carl Schurz, who was then a resident of Watertown, Wisconsin. In that city had settled, in 1855, a German by the name of Carl Siburg, whose wife had been a pupil of Froebel, and was an expert in the theory and practice of the Kindergarten. To her the Schurzes had sent their daughter, and Mrs. Schurz described to Miss Peabody the methods and results of her education. At once Miss Peabody was impressed with the beauty and the utility of this system, and sought in all directions for aids in comprehending it, securing one of Froebel's minor works as her guide. In 1860 she opened in Boston a school for little children on the basis of what she supposed was Froebel's system. This school became popular, and it was copied elsewhere. " In the course of the next ten years some innocent because ignorant, inadequate attempts were made at Kindergartens," she wrote in later years; " but without such study into the practical details of the method as to do any justice to Froebel's idea ; and on the whole the premature attempt was unfortunate. The most noted one was my own in Boston ; but I must do myself the justice to say that I discovered its radical deficiency by seeing that the results promised by Froebel, as the result of his method, did not accrue, but consequences that he deprecated, and which its financial success and the delight of the children and their parents in the pretty play-school did not beguile me into overlooking."

In 1867 Miss Peabody, after seven years of Kindergarten teaching in the imperfect manner she then knew, took the money she had secured from her lecturing under the auspices of Mrs. Quincy and went to Europe to study the system at first hand. "An hour in the Hamburg Kindergarten opened my eyes," she said afterwards. Having devoted a year to mastering Froebel's system she returned to Boston with the intention of raising money enough to bring to that city an expert Kindergartener. On her return she found that Mrs. Kriege and her daughter had opened a Kindergarten and a training-school in Boston the year before under the auspices of Mrs. Horace Mann. When they left the city to return to Germany, four years later,

they were succeeded by two of their pupils, Miss Garland
and Miss Weston. Marie Boelte opened a Kindergarten in
New York soon after, and as Mrs. Kraus-Boelte she trained
Miss Blow of St. Louis, and other expert Kindergarteners.
It will be seen, therefore, that the efforts of Miss Peabody
led directly to most of the chief Kindergarten labors in this
country. All the writers on the history of education have
recognized her important services in this direction. For instance, George H. Martin, in his "Evolution of the Massachusetts Public School System," says of her work : "The
apostle of the Kindergarten movement in Massachusetts
was Miss Peabody, and to her efforts with tongue and pen
is due whatever success the movement has had." In his
"History of Education in the United States," Richard G.
Boone justly says : "What Baroness Marenholtz-Bœlow
did for Europe, Miss Peabody has done for America. She
was the earliest, as she has been one of the most persistent,
advocates of its merits. Hers was the first literature on the
subject — hers a pioneer labor."

In May, 1873, Miss Peabody began the publication in
Boston of "The Kindergarten Messenger," a monthly magazine of twenty-four pages, which she continued to the end
of 1874. Then her Kindergarten contributions appeared for
one year in the "Journal of Education," but that arrangement
not proving satisfactory, the "Messenger" was resumed with
the first of 1875. It had a limited circulation, but Miss
Peabody gave to it devoted service, and made it a valuable
means of extending the Kindergarten method. In 1876,
the expense and labor proving too great for individual effort,
the magazine was surrendered to W N. Hailman, who
edited and published in Milwaukee "The New Education."
The work on "Moral Culture of Infancy and Kindergarten
Guide," which Miss Peabody had published in 1863, in connection with her sister, Mrs. Mary Mann, she repudiated
after her return from Europe "as an ignorant and abor-

tive attempt." She rewrote it, and in this revised form it became a means of bringing Froebel's method into wide recognition.

After 1868 Miss Peabody's life was largely devoted to the work of the Kindergarten, principally in lecturing and by means of her writings. In 1870 she gave an address in Chicago before the Society of Superintendents and Principals on "The Genuine Kindergarten versus Ignorant Attempts at it;" and she repeated it before the Wisconsin Teachers' Convention, as well as in Milwaukee, Cleveland, and other cities. Soon after returning from Germany she organized in Boston the Kindergarten Association, which proved a valuable ally to her labors. For many years she gave courses of lectures to Kindergarteners, and these were repeated in several of the leading cities of the country. She also organized the National Froebel Union. In 1886 she published "Letters to Kindergarteners," and in 1893 "Lectures in Training Schools for Kindergarteners." The Report of the Commissioner of Education for 1870 contained one of the first official recognitions of the Kindergarten in this country, being a paper by Miss Peabody on "The Necessity of Kindergarten Culture in our Systems of Public Instruction." In the same year she published a pamphlet "Plea for Froebel's Kindergarten as the First Grade of Primary Art Education." In Barnard's "Kindergarten and Culture Papers" appeared articles from her pen on "The Development of the Kindergarten in the United States," "Froebel's Principles and Methods in the Nursery," as well as other essays.

During the early years of her advocacy of the Kindergarten Miss Peabody lived for a time in Cambridge. Then she removed to Concord, where she was deeply interested in the sessions of the School of Philosophy, to which she gave several addresses. Afterwards she was again a resident of Boston, and then she went to Jamaica Plain, one of the rural suburbs of the city, where she died January

3, 1894. She planned to write her autobiography, but the failure of her eyesight made this task impossible of accomplishment. Much of the story of her early life was told in her " Reminiscences of Dr. Channing," which she published in 1877, a book that is most instructive for the whole early period of the transcendental movement. She was able to edit her lectures to Kindergarteners during her last years, and to bring together a number of her early writings, first printed in " The Dial " and the " Æsthetic Papers," under the title of " Last Evening with Allston, and other Papers," which was published in 1886.

The last enthusiasm of Miss Peabody was for the Indians, in whose behalf she devoted much effort with tongue and pen. She became the special champion of the interests of Sarah Winnemucca, by some strange perversion of knowledge called " Princess," by whom she was cheated and defrauded until she was rescued by her friends from the clutches of one who had grossly imposed upon her sympathies and her generosity. If in this instance deceived, Miss Peabody saw the real needs of the Indians and wisely advocated their cause. She desired for them an education that would fit them for an industrial and moral life.

With the transcendental movement from first to last Miss Peabody was familiar, being a most important part of it herself. She was intimate with Emerson, Margaret Fuller, who gave her first course of conversations in her West Street rooms, Theodore Parker, George Ripley, Alcott, Thoreau, James Freeman Clarke, and all the others of that noble company. She was attracted by Mazzini, Frederic Maurice, and the other leaders of liberal thought in Europe. She never tired of talking of these men or of commending their teachings to others. Always poor, always dependent upon her own exertions, she did more for others than for herself, and never failed to champion any cause that commended itself to her enthusiastic and heroic nature. Mrs.

Elizabeth P. Peabody

Ednah D. Cheney, who knew her long and well, has truly said of her: "She was a thorough transcendentalist, and worked with Emerson and Alcott and Parker in all that great movement. Her powers of conversation were large, although she was sometimes led by her enthusiasm for the causes or the people she loved into larger discourse than suited the occasion or the audience. These philanthropic interests turned her attention from literature, in which I think she might have taken a much higher position if she had been more swayed by personal and intellectual ambition." Mrs. Caroline H. Dall also justly estimated her merits and her defects when she wrote: "A woman of remarkable accumulations of learning, and as remarkable a breadth of sympathy. Her own great powers did not accomplish all they ought, because it was impossible for her to apply them systematically."

A beautiful tribute to the memory of Miss Peabody, who "literally gave herself to the cause" of the Kindergarten, was the establishment in the West End of Boston, in April, 1896, of the Elizabeth Peabody House, a settlement for Kindergarteners in one of the poorer districts of the city. For its maintenance was organized an Association of her friends and others interested in the teaching of the children of the slums. There her life of philanthropy, lofty thought, and childlike transparency is continued in her spirit of devotion to the good of others.

X

MEMBERS OF THE TRANSCENDENTAL CLUB

SEVERAL of the members of the transcendental club were not contributors to "The Dial." It may be desirable to say a word of each of them, as well as of a few persons who were connected with "The Dial" in an indirect manner. Few of these persons made a conspicuous place for themselves, and yet all of them are worthy of recognition. They were thoughtful, progressive, and earnest persons; and most of them had an interesting history.

The chairman of the transcendental club at most of its meetings, holding that position because of his seniority in age, was Convers Francis (1795–1863), who was minister of the First Parish in Watertown from 1819 to 1842, and professor of pulpit eloquence and pastoral care at the Harvard Divinity School from 1842 to 1863. He was the brother of Lydia Maria Child, who owed much to him in the way of mental culture and moral incentive. He wrote a life of John Eliot and other biographies. O. B. Frothingham said of him: "Though never conspicuous either as preacher or minister, and never recognized as a representative apostle, he was influential as a believer in the spiritual philosophy among young men. To him Theodore Parker acknowledged his debt; to him successive classes of divinity students owed the stimulus and direction that carried them into the transcendental ranks; Johnson, Longfellow, Higginson [and Frothingham] were his pupils at Cambridge, and carried thence ideas which he had shaped if not originated. He gave his full assent to the principles of intuitive philosophy, and used them

as the pillars of Christianity." His influence on the transcendental movement was considerable, and all the more
so because he was conservative and unaggressive.

One of the most remarkable persons connected with the
transcendental movement was Orestes Augustus Brownson
(1803–1876), who became a member of the Catholic Church
in 1844. He was the editor and publisher of the "Boston
Quarterly Review" from 1838 to 1842, and it was regarded
as a representative of transcendentalism, though it was
conspicuously marked by the peculiar qualities of its editor,
who wrote most of the articles contained in its pages.
It was afterward the organ of American Catholicism under
the name of "Brownson's Review." Brownson's name is
frequently mentioned in all accounts of the transcendental
period, partly because of his many changes in his beliefs
and in his denominational connections, and partly because
of his dogmatic and opinionated attitude on all questions
he discussed. He was a vigorous philosophical thinker,
embraced transcendentalism with ardor and defended it
with skill, and was ready to meet all antagonists in defence
of his opinions. At first a Presbyterian, then a Universalist, afterward a labor-reformer and discarder of all religious organizations, he became a Unitarian in Boston,
organized a society independent of all denominational connections, in order to Christianize working-men, and at last
found his rightful place in the Catholic Church. He was
as restless amongst Catholics as he was amongst Protes-
tants, severely criticised that church in this country, and
came under the condemnation of the church authorities
for his opinions and his want of submissiveness. In the
Catholic Church, however, he was in his right place,
for his dogmatism and his intense faith in supernaturalism
made that church the only one fitting his nature. In the
same way Thomas Hecker, for some months a student
at Brook Farm and at Alcott's Fruitlands, found his true

place in Catholicism; for he, too, was a believer in the supernatural in a way that Protestantism does not sanction in any of its higher forms. To these two men the Catholic Church owes a great debt for the American interpretation they gave its principles and its spirit. Brownson conducted his "Review" with ability, vigorous conviction, and rare versatility. Ripley's review of his earlier writings, contained in the first number of "The Dial," gives a friendly and just recognition to his talents, his literary skill, and his aggressive temper.

Another member of the transcendental club was Ephraim Peabody (1807–1856), minister of Unitarian churches in Meadville, Penn., Cincinnati (where he was connected with editing "The Western Messenger"), New Bedford, and of King's Chapel in Boston from 1846 to 1856. He was an excellent preacher, and the founder of the first organized system of charities in Boston. Cyrus A. Bartol (1813–1900) was the minister of the West Church in Boston from 1835 to 1888. He was a radical Unitarian of the more devout type, a strong and quaint preacher, one of the most original of the transcendentalists, and had a style as epigrammatic as Emerson's, and of remarkable vigor and raciness. The Free Religious Association was organized in his house, and he was deeply interested in its purposes. He published "Radical Problems," 1872; "The Rising Faith," 1874; "Principles and Portraits," 1880, and many other books and discourses. Nothing more fully in harmony with transcendentalism can be found than these books.

James Walker (1794–1874) was minister of the Unitarian Church in Charlestown (now a part of Boston) from 1818 to 1839. He then became the professor of moral and intellectual philosophy in Harvard College. He became the president in 1853, but resigned in 1860. He edited "The Christian Examiner," published two or three volumes of sermons, and edited several text-books in moral and mental science. He was an able preacher, a vigorous thinker, and a man of influence. He early accepted the spiritual philosophy, though he was not as loyal to it as Alcott and others desired. The more enthusiastic features of transcendentalism were not acceptable to him, his attitude being that of Ripley and Hedge rather than that of Alcott and Emerson.

One of the less frequent attendants upon the meetings of the transcendental club was Nathaniel L. Frothingham (1793-1870), the father of O. B. Frothingham, who was minister of the First Church in Boston from 1815 to 1850. He was an able preacher, a poet of some ability, one of the earliest students of German, and a man of delightful character. His life has been written by his son, in his "Boston Unitarianism." Caleb Stetson was graduated at Harvard in 1822 and died in 1870. He was for many years the minister of the Unitarian church in Medford, and a man of wit, learning, and most genial character. He was a loyal transcendentalist, and friendly to Parker and the other radicals in the days of controversy and criticism. George Putnam, who joined with Emerson, Ripley, and Hedge in the first meeting of the "like-minded," that resulted in the organization of the transcendental club, but was not present after the first meeting, was for many years the minister of the First Parish in Roxbury (now a part of Boston), and one of the most eloquent and popular of the Unitarian ministers. He was of the older school of Unitarians, and had no interest in the transcendental movement.

William Russell and LeBaron Russell were Boston physicians, graduates of Harvard and its medical school. The latter aided Emerson in editing Carlyle's miscellaneous writings, in 1834; and he was very active in securing aid for Emerson after the burning of his house, in 1872. Jonathan Phillips was a relative of Wendell Phillips, a wealthy Boston mer-

chant, a parishioner of Dr. Channing, and one of his most
confidential friends, aiding him largely in his charities.
Dr. Channing attended one meeting of the transcendental
club, with which he was warmly in sympathy. He did not
take a more active part in it doubtless because his health
compelled him to reserve his strength and to withhold himself from most public meetings of every kind. George Bancroft also attended one meeting, but he was an idealist, and
largely in sympathy with the transcendentalists. That he did
not attend regularly was probably owing to his residence in
the western part of the State at the period of the club's
activity.

Charles Follen was born in Germany in 1796, graduated
at Giessen, became a lecturer there, but was obliged to leave
Germany because of his liberal political views, and went to
Paris. In 1820 the French government ordered all foreigners
from the country, and he took up his residence in Zurich,
and became professor of Latin in the cantonal schools of the
Grisons. He was soon made professor of civil law in the
University of Basel, and he edited the literary journal of the
university. In 1824 Russia, Austria, and Prussia demanded
his surrender for disseminating revolutionary doctrines, and
he fled to America. He studied theology with Dr. Channing,
whose intimate friend he became, and he was made instructor
in ecclesiastical history in the Harvard Divinity School. In
1830 he was made the professor of German literature in
Harvard College. He identified himself with the anti-
slavery movement, and in 1834 Harvard refused to continue his professorship. He preached and lectured, tutored
boys, was for a time minister of a Unitarian church in
New York, and in 1839 was settled over a church in the
east village of Lexington. Returning from New York,
where he was delivering a course of lectures on German
literature, he perished on the steamer Lexington, which
was burned January 3, 1840. His wife, Eliza Lee Cabot,

one of the first writers of books for children, published his biography, together with a complete edition of his works. He was an able psychologist, and left a partly completed work on that science.

Sarah Alden Bradford was born in Boston, July 31, 1793. She married Samuel Ripley, son of Dr. Ezra Ripley of Concord, who married the grandmother of Emerson, having succeeded her first husband as the Concord minister. Samuel Ripley was minister of the Unitarian church in Waltham for twenty-eight years, and during this period he kept a boys' school in his house, his wife teaching the advanced Greek and Latin. In 1846 the Ripleys moved to Concord, and occupied the Old Manse, thus causing Hawthorne to leave that historic house. Mrs. Ripley died there, July 26, 1867, her husband having died in 1847. She was a member of the transcendental club, the only woman besides Margaret Fuller and Elizabeth Peabody. She was a much better educated person than either of them, and was capable of conducting her pupils through all the studies of Harvard College in her day. " She became one of the best Greek scholars in the country," Emerson said of her, and he was her pupil, as were his brothers, " and continued in her latest years the habit of reading Homer, the tragedians, and Plato. But her studies took a wide range in mathematics, in natural philosophy, in theology, as well as in ancient and modern literature. She had always a keen ear open to whatever new facts astronomy, chemistry, or the theories of light and heat had to furnish. Any knowledge, all knowledge, was welcome. Her stores increased day by day. She was absolutely without pedantry. Nobody ever heard of her learning until a necessity came for its use, and then nothing could be more simple than her solution of the problem proposed to her. The most intellectual gladly conversed with one whose knowledge, however rich and varied, was always with her only the means of new acquisition." " A wonderful attraction she was," wrote Dr. F. H. Hedge, "independently of her rare acquirements, which might draw the scholar to seek the converse of so learned a woman, — an attraction proceeding from no personal charms, but due to the astonishing vivacity, the *all-aliveness*, of her presence, which made it impossible to imagine her otherwise than wide-awake and active in word or work. The charm of her society to me was her perfect naturalness, the utter unconsciousness of any special claim to attention based on her superior learning, which was never intruded, and only came to light when some student or savant wished to compare notes with her or she with him. Otherwise, the woman entirely absorbed and concealed the scholar. It was the woman, not the scholar, that attracted, that edified, and — joined with the generous hospitality and manly qualities of her husband — made their house at Waltham so delightful a place to visit for all who were privileged to be their guests." That Mrs. Ripley was a convinced and loyal transcendentalist appears in a letter she wrote to her son-in-law, Rev. George F. Simmons, in April, 1845 : "Religion has become so simple a matter to me, — a yearning after God, an earnest desire for the peace that flows from the consciousness of union with him. It is the last thought that floats through my mind as I sleep, the first that comes when I wake. It forms the basis of my present life, saddened by past experience. It bedims my eyes with tears when I walk out into the beautiful nature, where love is all around me. And yet no direct ray comes to my soul. Perhaps it is God's peace instead of God I seek ; so I sit and wait in patience for his grace, and will still wait. Earnests and foretastes come ; but humble waiting in days of darkness will, I trust, bring better fruits." Mrs. Ripley's biography was written by Elizabeth Hoar for "Worthy Women of Our First Century," and it contains many reminiscences of Emerson and the other members of the transcendental club.

George Partridge Bradford, a brother of Mrs. Ripley, was a member of the transcendental club and also of the Brook Farm Association. He was born in Boston, February 16, 1807, and was prepared for college by his sister. He graduated at Harvard in 1825, and three years later from the Divinity School. He never preached, transcendentalism making that impossible for him. He was a teacher all his life thereafter, in Concord, Plymouth, and elsewhere. He was a true scholar, a devoted friend, and a man of sterling worth, albeit very modest and unpretentious. He was spoken of with admiration by all the transcendental set, who loved the man and believed in him. He edited a volume of translations from Fénelon, and he completed the brief history of philosophic thought in Boston, begun by George Ripley for the "Memorial History of Boston," and left unfinished on his death. Bradford died January 26, 1890. While living in the Old Manse at Concord, Hawthorne wrote to Margaret Fuller: "I have thought of receiving a personal friend, and a man of delicacy, into my household, and have taken a step towards that object. But in doing so I was influenced far less by what Mr. Bradford is than by what he is not; or, rather, his negative qualities seem to take away his personality, and leave his excellent characteristics to be fully and fearlessly enjoyed. I doubt whether he be not precisely the rarest man in the world." George William Curtis said of him: "A more gentle, truthful, generous, constant, high-minded, accomplished man could not be known. However wide and various and delightful your acquaintance may have been, if you knew George Bradford, you knew a man unlike all others. His individuality was entirely unobtrusive, but it was absolute. His admirable mind, the natural loftiness of his aim, his instinctive sympathy with every noble impulse and humane endeavor, his fine intellectual cultivation, all made him the friend of the best men and women of his time and neighborhood, and none among them but acknowledged the singular charm of a companion who asserted his convictions by his character, and with whom controversy was impossible. Mr. Bradford had the temperament, the tastes, and the acquirements of a scholar; a fondness for nature, a knowledge of which made him her interpreter; yet still more obvious were the social sympathy and tenderness of feeling that brought him into intimate personal relations which time could not touch."

Robert Bartlett, a native of Plymouth, was one of the younger members of the transcendental club. He graduated at Harvard in 1836, was a tutor in the college, and died in 1843. In the oration he gave at Harvard, in 1839, on the occasion of receiving his master's degree, he made a very positive statement of his faith in transcendentalism. It attracted much admiration, gained for the author a permanent reputation amongst the transcendentalists, and was published in Heraud's "Monthly Magazine," in April, 1840. In this oration Bartlett said: "We do not express the men and the miracles of our history in our social action, and correspondingly, ay, and by consequence, we do not outwrite them in poetry or art. We are looking abroad and back after a literature. Let us come and live, and know in living a high philosophy and faith; so shall we find now, here, the elements, and in our own souls the fire. Of every storied bay and cliff and plain, we will make something infinitely nobler than Salamis or Marathon. This pale Massachusetts sky, this sandy soil and raw wind, all shall nurture us. Rich skies, fair fields, shall come to us, suffused with the immortal hues of spirit, of beauteous act and thought. Unlike all the world before us, our own age and land shall be classic to ourselves." Charles A. Dana addressed a sonnet to Bartlett in the next to the last number of "The Dial."

In the first number of the third volume of "The Dial," Emerson gave an account of the Chardon Street Bible Convention, held in Boston in the winter of 1840–41 ; and he published in full " the best speech made on that occasion," that of Nathaniel H. Whiting, of South Marshfield, Mass. "Himself a plain unlettered man," Emerson wrote, " leaving for the day a mechanical employment to address his fellows, he possessed eminent gifts for success in assemblies so constituted. He has fluency, self-command, an easy, natural method, and a very considerable power of statement. No one had more entirely the ear of his audience." A shoemaker, and devoted to his calling, Mr. Whiting improved his intellectual gifts by reading, and by such means of culture as came in his way. He was interested in the associationist movement, and took an active part in its conferences and other gatherings, though he was not a member of any community. He was also a faithful anti-slavery worker. He was a prominent citizen of Marshfield, a member of the State legislature, and for a number of years was connected with the Custom House in Boston. He was a representative come-outer in religion, and greatly interested in theological questions. He recently died in Marshfield, respected and honored by all who knew him.

In the first number of the third volume of " The Dial," Emerson published an article on " Prayers." He gave four original compositions of that kind, and said that " the last of the four orisons is written in a singularly calm and healthful spirit." This was the work of Junius Alcott, a younger brother of Amos B. Alcott. He lived in Alcott's house in Concord during his absence in England in the year 1842. He attended the Bible Convention in Boston, and then resided at Oriskany, N. Y.

In the third number of the third volume of " The Dial " Charles Lane reviewed " An Essay on Transcendentalism," published in Boston, in 1842. This pamphlet was written by Charles Ellis of West Roxbury, a member of Theodore Parker's congregation, and one of his most intimate and devoted friends. He was a farmer and business man, well educated, a student and thinker, and thoroughly radical in religion after Parker's type. He was a representative transcendentalist, as that form of thought influenced practical men, and made them critics of the old forms of thought, and come-outers from the old forms of religion.

In his diary, when Emerson recorded that he must assume the responsibility of life or death for "The Dial," he wrote that he did not like "The Plain Speaker" so well as "The Edinburgh Review." "The spirit of the last may be conventional and artificial, but that of the first is coarse, sour, indigent; dwells in a cellar-kitchen and goes to make suicides." "The Plain Speaker" was noticed at the end of the fifth number of "The Dial" in a much more friendly spirit, possibly from the pen of Margaret Fuller. This journal was published in Providence, and edited by Christopher Greene and William M. Chace, who lived at Holly Home, two miles north of the city, in North Providence. In 1841 they invited Alcott to settle with them, offering to build him a cottage if he would do so. He described Holly Home in a letter to his brother Junius as "a charming retreat," and added : "I passed a week there lately, and was much pleased with the place and people." In Providence there was a considerable group of admirers of Alcott, and a school conducted on his principles, founded by Hiram Fuller, in which Margaret Fuller taught from 1837 to 1839. William Chace was the secretary of the Bible Convention held in Boston in 1841, of which Edmund Quincy was the president. Christopher Greene was one of the Friends of Universal Reform who met in the Chardon Street Chapel, Boston, in 1840, others being Garrison, Parker, W. H. Channing, Quincy, and Maria Chapman. Greene became a member of the Fruitlands community, thus showing his devotion to Alcott. He married Chace's sister, who may have been the Sarah A. Chace who wrote the poem copied from " The Plain Speaker " into " The Dial " at the end of the notice already mentioned. " The Plain Speaker " seems to have been a radical journal of the most revolutionary reforms, and therefore was not acceptable to Emerson.

XI

CRITICISMS AND CARICATURES OF THE DIAL

THE fervor of its writers, the air of having something to say that outsiders could not appreciate, and the unconcern for facts and literary laws that marked some of its writers, made "The Dial" a source of ridicule to those not in sympathy with its high purpose and its earnest spiritual conviction. Even its friends could not but smile at the extravagances of some of its writers, for the period was one of excess and *naïveté*. To those who did not receive the gospel of newness and freedom, there was occasion in its pages for much of ridicule and sarcasm. Especially were the "Orphic Sayings" of Alcott, and the prose rhapsody by Charles Newcomb, called "Dolon," held up to scorn and laughed at to excess. By its unfriendly critics nothing too severe could be said against a journal so opposed to the customary in literature as was "The Dial." The editor of the "Boston Times" quite exhausted his ingenuity in ridiculing it: "It is, to us, humble uninitiated sinners, yet ignorant of the sublime 'mysteries,' one of the most transcendentically (we like big words) ridiculous productions." The "Boston Post" spoke of its "dreamy, silly, Carlyle-imitating style of writing," and said it was "rich in the profoundly allegorical and hopelessly obscure." Yet this newspaper praised some of the numbers for their freshness, high-toned sentiment, and truly American spirit.

Although a member of the transcendental club, and at this time to a considerable extent in sympathy with its members, yet Orestes A. Brownson was too much a dogmatist and too thoroughly a philosophical iconoclast to spare his friends of " The Dial." In the " Boston Quarterly Review " for January, 1841, of which he was the editor and to a large extent the writer, he said of the first two numbers : " This magazine has already acquired a reputation ; and it promises to exert no inconsiderable influence on the thought and literature of our country. It may be regarded, we suppose, as the organ of the Transcendentalists or exquisites of the movement party, — radicals, indeed, of a most ultra stamp, who would radicalize in kid gloves and satin slippers. The Dialists belong to the genus *cullotic*, and have no fellowship with your vulgar *sans-cullotic*.

" The opening address of the editors to their readers [by Emerson] is unnecessarily offensive. . . . ' The Dial ' contains pieces in prose and verse, and in general inserts its poetry in its prose, and its prose in its rhymes. . . . ' The Problem ' [by Emerson] is not merely verse, it is poetry, and unsurpassed, if equalled, by any production of the American muse with which we are acquainted. ' Wood Notes ' [also by Emerson] are passable, but they fall far short of the sweet, wild, sad music every true lover of nature hears whenever he walks in the woods. . . .

" Of this magazine we may say in general it is a truly remarkable work. It is full of rich thought, though somewhat injured by its puerile conceits and childish expressions. Its thought is in general superior to its expression. Its authors seem to have caught some partial glimpses, and to have felt the movings of a richer, a higher life, which carries them away, and which as yet they have not been able to master. To our taste they want robustness, manliness, and practical aims. They are too vague, evanescent, aerial ; but nevertheless, there is a ' sad sincerity ' about many of them ; and one cannot help feeling that these after all are the men and women who are to shape our future. On many sides they expose themselves to ridicule, but at bottom there is a serious, solemn purpose of which

even they are but half conscious. Though we often find
them too ultra for our belief, and sometimes too finical
for our taste, yet we view their movement with deep interest, and hope from their labors much to lead to a new and
higher life for the individual and for the world."

This criticism was in the main sound, for it is doubtless
true that "The Dial" was open to the objections urged by
Brownson. Even the "New York Tribune," edited by Horace
Greeley, who was most friendly to "The Dial" and what it
represented, had its word of reservation in regard to some
of its teachings. In a notice printed January 14, 1842, it
has this generous word of praise : "Some of the speculations indulged in this magazine will jar on the general ear ;
but there has never been a periodical in this country so
replete with elevated Thought and profound Spiritualism as
'The Dial.'" The number for July 15, 1843, contained a
reprint of Emerson's paper entitled "Past and Present," published in the July number of that year. In noticing this
number it was said that this paper presented "an original
view of a most original work [Carlyle's], full of acuteness
and insight, yet scarcely rating the book so highly as it
deserves." Of "The Great Lawsuit," by Margaret Fuller, it
said : "It sparkles with striking thoughts and noble sentiments, yet to many readers it will seem too diffuse, and to
lack directness. None can study it, however, without being
instructed thereby and elevated." The next number published a long extract from Margaret Fuller's article, which
was introduced with the statement that it combined "remarkable justness of sentiment with brilliancy of expression.
There is but one woman in America who could have written it."

Another friendly critic of "The Dial" was "The Western
Messenger," of Louisville, edited by James Freeman Clarke
and other contributors to "The Dial." In a notice of the
second number that journal defended its aims and spirit,

but it concluded by saying: "Thus far, to speak frankly, we do not think they [the editors] have shown the power they possess. The articles in the number before us, if we except two or three, will, we think, do little good. However, we know that among the writers for this work are some dozen of the purest, cleanest, and truest minds in the land, and such as will be felt, and felt deeply." In the last number of "The Western Messenger," that for April, 1841, was this notice: "We have said not a word of 'The Dial,' for we are slow to praise our own family, and the writers in this periodical are our dear friends. Therefore one word only. Readers! Believe not the Geese, who have hissed their loudest at this new-comer. Such foolish creatures cannot save the capitol. 'The Dial' marks an Era in American literature; it is the wind-flower of a new spring in the Western world. For profound thought, a pure tone of personal and social morality, wise criticisms, and fresh beauty, 'The Dial' has never been equalled in America. Subscribe for it as you love yourselves."

The editors of "The Western Messenger," however, were fully cognizant of the limitations of the writers in "The Dial." Friendly as they were towards their transcendentalist brethren, they were fully alive to what was excessive and ridiculous in their writings. Especially was this true of James Freeman Clarke, and of Christopher P. Cranch, who edited the "Messenger" in June, 1837, and for four months at the end of 1838 and beginning of 1839. These two transcendentalists amused themselves with drawing caricatures of the "Dial" writers and sayings. One of these represents a man lying on a bed sipping wine, a copy of "The Dial" having fallen to the floor, while his wife sits at the foot of the bed blacking his boots. This was called "The Moral Influence of 'The Dial,'" and it had this legend from the poem on "Life" by Ellery Channing, contained in the third number of the third volume:

> " Why for work art thou striving,
> Why seek'st thou for aught ?
> To the soul that is living
> All things shall be brought."

The same poem led to the production of another sketch, representing an immense man, with a copy of "The Dial" sticking from his coat-tail pocket, watching two companions of like dimensions near him. All utter the following sentiment to a lean and cadaverous man gazing on them with amazement expressed on his features :

> " Greatly to be
> Is enough for me,
> Is enough for thee."

In one of the cleverest of these sketches Cranch represented Margaret Fuller as driving a carriage, and Emerson as riding behind her. The editors are presented as saying :

> " Our Dial shows the march of light
> O'er forests, hills, and meadows."

To this a critic, trudging by, replies :

> " Not so, and yet you name it right ;
> It marks the flight of shadows."

These witty persons shot their shafts at higher game than "The Dial" writers, and did not spare Emerson. In one of their sketches appears a bare-foot rustic, with a great eye-ball for a head, and gazing over hills and valleys, illustrating Emerson's saying in his little book on "Nature": " Standing on the bare ground, I become a transparent eyeball." A man with an immense melon-body, sitting in the midst of melons and corn in a field, is a caricature of this sentence in the same work : " I expand and live in the warm day, like corn and melons." Other sketches they made, but a few of the sentences which excited their mirth will show the drift of them all: "The great man angles with himself; he needs no other bait." "They are contented to be brushed like flies from the path of the great man." "The man has never lived who can feed us ever." "We are lined with eyes. We see with our feet." In one of these sketches Andrews Norton is represented as addressing the alumni of the Harvard Divinity School, and saying: "The dwellers in the region of shadows complain that the earth is not substantial enough for them to stand upon. The last sect of infidels is those who deny miracles, and yet profess themselves to be Christians." One listener says, "That's true;" another, "That's good, give it to 'em!" and yet another, "Rather strong! it might be qualified." This was intended to satirize Norton's attacks upon Ripley and Emerson. Yet another of the sketches represents Theodore Parker as rushing, with eager haste, towards a collection of books, while the owner holds up both hands in amazement, and two dogs are yelping after the assiduous book-worm. The title is: "Theodore Parker's supposed delight in visiting a book-store or library in Germany." These sketches have never been published, but James Freeman Clarke had a portfolio of thirty of them, which is now in the possession of his family. This portfolio bears the title, "Illustrations of the New Philosophy, 1835. By C. P. Cranch." This date can only refer to the time when the first of these sketches were made, for the latest of them could not have been made earlier than April, 1843.

In a personal letter Cranch said of his part in the production of these sketches: "I don't remember that Clarke made any drawings, but he sometimes suggested them. I think it was his idea first, that of illustrating some of the quaint sayings of Emerson. With regard to the two sketches first mentioned, I am quite sure I never conceived or drew them or suggested any such matters. If I drew them I have entirely forgotten it. It was not Clarke but myself who drew

Miss Fuller driving the carriage, but I had nothing to do with those mottoes. But I confess to the scraps, 'The Transparent Eyeball,' and the 'Corn and Melons,' also 'The Great Man brushing away the Flies.' It was not, however, 'The Dial' writers that we then caricatured, for 'The Dial' did not appear till 1840, and it was in 1839 that I was in the West. It should be stated, too, that these and subsequent sketches were not intended as anything more than humorous attempts to put into a literal form on paper some of Emerson's quaint sentences. There was no one else I tried my hand on at that time; and the first things I did in that way were really more for the private amusement of Clarke and myself and a few other Emersonians, and there never was any intention that they should be known to the public. And I always took pains to repudiate any Philistine idea that anything like ridicule was here attempted."

It is not probable that anything published in the newspapers or reviews had much effect upon the circulation of "The Dial." However much their comments may have amused the general public, they did not lessen the number of transcendentalists. The fact is that "The Dial" had but a small constituency at the best, for its writers had not yet created their public. The new generation had not yet been educated that would accept their teachings with confidence.

XII

SUCCESSORS TO THE DIAL

It cannot be said that "The Dial" alone marked the hours of the day when it was published. It had a number of contemporaries and successors that were not wholly unlike itself, however widely they may have differed from it in some respects. Especially was this true of the journals edited or contributed to by those who wrote for "The Dial" itself. "The Dial" was not the only journal to give welcome to transcendentalism, for we have seen that it was not wholly unknown to the pages of "The Christian Examiner." At an even earlier date than "The Dial" itself had been published "The Western Messenger" as an organ of the Unitarian churches west of the Alleghanies.

The full name of this monthly magazine was "The Western Messenger; devoted to Religion and Literature," and the first number appeared at Cincinnati, in June, 1835, five years in advance of "The Dial." It was continued in Cincinnati for eight months, when it was removed to Louisville, where it was published until April, 1841. It was under the editorial care of William H. Channing and James H. Perkins during the period of its Cincinnati existence; but after it went to Louisville James Freeman Clarke was the controlling editor. Ephraim Peabody, C. P. Cranch, and William G. Eliot had more or less intimate editorial connection with it. Among the other Unitarian ministers who contributed to it were Samuel Osgood, Charles T. Brooks, and John S. Dwight.

"The Western Messenger" was distinctly a Unitarian periodical, and was largely devoted to the furtherance of the interests of that denomination. It was to a considerable degree literary in its inclinations, however, and it gave much attention to reforms. It was a vigorous advocate of the anti-slavery movement, considering the time and place of its publication. It was also distinctly inclined to transcendentalism, Clarke having been a member of the transcendental club and in sympathy with its attitude on philosophical and religious questions. He invited Margaret Fuller and Emerson to contribute to the pages of " The Western Messenger," which they did on several occasions. In this journal first appeared Emerson's " Each and All," " The Humble-Bee," " The Rhodora," and " Good-bye, Proud World!" Alcott was also a contributor, and Jones Very gave it a large number of his poems. William D. Gallagher printed in it many of his verses.

The attitude of Clarke and his contributors towards transcendentalism was not only friendly, but it was appreciative, if not wholly receptive of its teachings. This may be seen in an article which appeared in November, 1838, in which the editor commented on Mr. Emerson and the New School, anent the Divinity School Address of the previous July. "To confess the truth," wrote James Freeman Clarke, "when we received and read the address, we did not discover anything objectionable at all. We were quite delighted with it. We read it, to be sure, looking for good and not evil, and we found enough that was good to satisfy us. Parts seemed somewhat obscure, and for that we were sorry — in places we felt hurt by the phraseology, but we bounded carelessly over these rocks of offence and pitfalls, enjoying the beauty, sincerity, and magnanimity of the general current of the address." Immediately following this article, in the same number, was one on " The New School in Literature," probably from the same pen, in which the fullest sympathy with transcendentalism was expressed. "There is a large and increasing number of the clergy and laity," this article said, "of thinking men and educated women, especially of the youth in our different colleges, of all sects and all professions, who are dissatisfied with the present state of religion, philosophy, and literature. The common principle which binds them together, and makes them if you choose a school, is a desire for more of life, soul, energy, originality, in these great departments of thought. If they like Carlyle, it is not that they agree wholly with his opinions, or think his style perfect, but because they find in him a genuine man, full of life and originality. If they listen with delight to Mr. Emerson, and read his works with pleasure, it is not that they agree with all his speculations, but that they sympathize with his independence, manliness, and freedom. . . . In a word, they esteem genuine, earnest, independent thought as the one thing needful in our whole life, and where they find this in a man they are drawn towards him by strong sympathies, wherever there is reality and not appearance, substance and not form, living energy and not hollow show, sincere conviction and not traditional cant — there they feel their chief wants met and answered. . . . Their sympathies embrace the secluded scholar, the active preacher, the devoted schoolmaster, the enthusiastic artist, the true poet — every man who feels that life should not be a mechanical routine, but be filled with earnestness, soul, and spiritual energy. All who look and hope and labor for something better than now is, who believe in progress, who trust in future improvement, and are willing to spend and be spent in bringing forward that better time, all such are members of the New School." These words would have been quite in place on the pages of "The Dial," and they anticipated much that was printed in that journal.

In the next to the last number of "The Western Messenger" there was printed an article on "Transcendentalism" from the pen of C. P. Cranch, which indicates how readily its pages were given to the interpretation of the teachings of that school, and to their advocacy. "The true transcen-

dentalism," Cranch said, " is that living and always new
spirit of truth, which is ever going forth on its conquests
into the world. . . . It is God himself, walking in his garden in the cool of the day. It is the Eternal Spirit breathing down on us the life-giving breeze of Almighty Grace.
. . . It is not ourselves. It is not the property of this man
or that woman, to be parcelled out in prismatic glimmer-
ings, and be bought and sold like earthly possessions. It
is the common delight of the mind. It is eminently the
spirit of earnest, free, large enquiry. . . . It does not con-
fine itself to opinions, but extends to great and good acts.
It is seen in the practical developments of our religion. It
is not the bare spirit of denial and doubt, but of yearning
faith also."

Such a " Dial " as some of the contributors to that peri-
odical desired was edited by William Henry Channing,
beginning with September, 1843, and ending with April,
1844. Its chief contributors had been writing for " The
Dial," including Channing himself. Among the others were
J. R. Lowell, G. W. Curtis, Margaret Fuller, Lydia Maria
Child, Charles A. Dana, C. P. Cranch, Ellery Channing,
A. B. Alcott, and Charles Lane. This journal was called
" The Present," was published monthly, and contained
thirty-six pages of " The Dial " size. After the first two all
were double numbers, and contained seventy-two pages.
With the twelfth number " The Present " was discontinued,
because the editor had undertaken " the near and sacred
duty " of writing a memoir of his uncle, Dr. Channing.
This volume of four hundred and thirty-two pages is one of
the most interesting in the history of reform publications in
this country. While it was distinctly in harmony with
transcendentalism, its chief mission was to advocate the
teachings of Fourier. Many articles were translated from
the French advocates of Fourierism, especially Leroux
and Considerant. A series of articles by the editor, con-

tinued through all the numbers of " The Present," presented
his own theories of social reconstruction. These were more
in harmony with what has been called Christian Socialism
than with the full details of Fourier's system.

Channing was too thoroughly a transcendentalist to accept
without reserve the mechanical theories of Fourier, or to
believe that the putting of a company of persons into a
phalanstery would re-form them into true men and women.
On the last page of the journal he said: "This periodical
was called 'The Present' as a means of suggesting that
this age, as all ages have been, is hallowed by the inspiration
and providence of God. The first hope of its editor was to
aid in awakening a more joyful confidence in the designs of
Heaven and the destinies of Humanity." Here his transcendentalism showed itself, as it did in his insistence that
the kingdom of God of the really spiritual Christian believer
affords the true ground of reform for those desiring a juster
and wiser human society. This is seen in the second article of
the first number, which was Channing's Credo, or confession
of faith. "I believe that the reign of Christ," he declared,
" shall be universal, and shall organize the now warring and
scattered nations into one holy society, where justice, wisdom, joy, shall harmonize the external world and crowd it
with countless varieties of beautiful productions; that the
central power of this kingdom of heaven is holiness, the
indwelling spirit of God."

Although so thoroughly a Christian socialist, yet Channing was one of the chief advocates of the change by which
Brook Farm became a Fourierite community. At a meeting held in Boston during the last days of 1843 the claims
of Fourierism were discussed at great length, and with the
result that Brook Farm went over to Fourier. The fullest
report of that meeting is contained in " The Present," and
was written by Channing himself. It gives more fully than
did Miss Peabody in " The Dial " the trend of the discus-

sion, as well as the practical results at which the meeting arrived. It also gave in full the list of officers of this convention, together with the resolutions which it adopted. In this article he said of the convention that it "marked an era in the history of New England." His theoretical position may be understood by a brief extract: "For the fulfilment of man's earthly destiny — unity with God and Man and Nature — the first condition is the organization of society according to the law of love. We are members one of another. Each human society, organized of various individuals, differing in character, intellect, energy, should form a Man; the harmoniously conspiring and co-laboring nations of the earth should form One Grand Man; and then God will inspire each man, and all men wholly, and Nature own our sovereignty."

To "The Present" Margaret Fuller contributed the sketch called "The Two Herberts," and Lydia Child furnished three articles. Lowell, Cranch, and Ellery Channing each contributed a number of poems. Alcott furnished two series of his "Sayings." Parke Godwin wrote in it a number of articles on social questions, in commendation of the associative principles. George William Curtis furnished an article on "Music and Ole Bull" to the last number. In the third number appeared the following poem from the pen of Charles A. Dana: —

AD ARMA!

Oh, loiterer, that dalliest with thy dreams,
    Content to watch thyself in graceful ease,
      While clang of steel burdens each passing breeze,
And all the air is radiant with its gleams;
Where noble hearts, as noble hearts beseems,
Answer the world's great cry with earnest deeds,
Fulfilling thus their own most inward needs;
Is there no Spartan nerve in all thy frame
    That feels the summons to that solemn field?
    And canst thou then its sacred honors yield,

And the high guerdon of eternal fame,
For purple skies and wreaths of fading flowers,
And the short lustre of these flitting hours ?

" The Present" also contained the following poems from
the pen of James Russell Lowell, which do not appear in
his collected works : —

WINTER.

The bird sings not in winter-time,
  Nor doth the happy murmur of the bees
Swarm round us from the chill, unleav'd lime ;
And shall ye hear the poet o' sunny rhyme,
  'Mid souls more bleak and bare than winter trees ?

As a lone singing bird that far away,
  Hath follow'd north the fickle smiles of spring,
Is ambush'd by a sudden bitter day,
And sits forlorn upon a leafless spray,

  Hiding his head beneath his numbed wing,
So is the poet, if he chance to fall
  'Mong hearts by whom he is not understood,
Dull hearts, whose throbbing grows not musical,
  Although their strings are blown upon by all
The sweetest breezes of the true and good.

His spirit pineth orphan'd of that home
  Wherein was nursed its wondrous infancy,
And whence sometimes 'neath night's all quiet dome,
Swiftly a winged memory will come,
  And prophesy of glory yet to be.

Then knows he that he hath not been exiled
  From those wide halls his own by right of birth ;
But hath been sent, a well-beloved child,
A chosen one on whom his father smiled,
  And blest, to be his messenger on Earth.

Then doth his brow with its right glory shine,
  And stretching forth his strong, undaunted wings,
He soareth to an atmosphere divine,
Whence he can see afar that clime benign,
  His fatherland, whose mystic song he sings.

So in his eyes there doth such blessing grow
That all those faces, erst so hard and dull,
With a sweet warmth of brotherhood do glow,
As he had seen them glisten long ago,
In that old home so free and beautiful.

SONNET

Therefore think not the Past is wise alone,
For Yesterday knows nothing of the Best,
And thou shalt love it as the nest
Whence glory-winged things to Heaven have flown:
To the great Soul alone are all things known ;
Present and future are to her as past,
While she in glorious madness doth forecast
That perfect bud, which seems a flower full-blown
To each new Prophet, and yet always opes
Fuller and fuller with each day and hour,
Heartening the soul with odor of fresh hopes,
And longings high, and gushings of wide power,
Yet never is or shall be fully blown
Save in the forethought of the Eternal One.

Transcendentalism being to a large degree individualistic
in its tendencies, it was more or less fully accepted by those
of various and antagonistic ways of thinking on religious,
social, and literary questions. Especially did the socialistic
movement of the time divide those who were in sympathy
with it from those who adhered strictly to the individualistic
spirit which transcendentalism fostered. That there was a
real difference of opinion between the individualists and the
associationists may be fully recognized by calling to mind
Emerson's sharp criticisms of Brook Farm and the kindred
communities of the day. In "The Harbinger," the organ
of Brook Farm, may be found what was to be said on the
other side. In a long and appreciative review of Emerson's
first volume of "Poems," John S. Dwight distinctly condemned them because of their lack of the spirit of human
sympathy and brotherhood. "But now," he wrote, "for the

humanity of these poems; what passion of the soul inspired
them? Alas! it is cold beauty; they yield no warmth, although they brace and invigorate you like December air;
they shine aloft, serene, august, resplendent like Orion on
a frosty night, and like him cold and distant; they counsel
loneliness, and call that true life."

An article from the pen of Charles A. Dana in the first volume of "The Harbinger" brings out keenly this antagonism
between the strict transcendentalists and the associationists.
In reviewing Eliza Thayer Clapp's "Studies in Religion"
he took occasion to criticise the transcendentalists severely,
giving the book only scantiest notice. As Miss Clapp was
then an ardent disciple of Emerson, Dana evidently aimed
his blow at the master and not at the pupil. As defining
the attitude of the associationists his words may be presented at some length: "Like many things beside in these
times this sect of thinkers has quite different values, if
we consider it as an element or as an individual thing.
Taken as a sign of dissatisfaction with the unpoetic and
even decaying husks which have been and in some quar-
ters still are not stintedly fed out, and of the deep impulse
to demand and to have something better, it commands our
sympathy and admiration. In the general *elan* towards
a broader mental freedom, it has contributed not a little.
Equally useful has been its part in the culture of some
of the best minds, who are now not only sitting by their
studious lamps, musing, searching, revolving new notions
and ideas wherewith to present, as with their homage and
their fealty, the approaching reformation, but who in truth
and in earnest have laid their hands to the work. Nor has
it been without service in the advancement of truth itself.
Amidst the brilliant paradoxes and glittering errors which
its Coryphæus, eminently a one-sided and unbalanced man
vainly endeavoring after equilibrium, from time to time
sends forth, are many great and wise ideas set to such

music that they cannot soon be forgotten. But regarded as a system of philosophy and ethics, the theory of our transcendentalists is fatally defective and erroneous. Briefly, it knows nothing of the progressive, hierarchical order of the universe, and by consequence stumbles at almost every step, and does not always stumble forwards. But we have neither space nor time for a scientific analysis; we only point out the prominent peculiarities of the system we speak of, for system it is, though it may not always be easy to perceive it. The chief of these is the want of real human sympathies. Its doctrine and tendency are extreme individualism. It sunders the man from his fellows, and even doubts whether it is necessary that he should have any fellows at all. In a word, it teaches a perfect spiritual selfishness. It is the poetic and mystical expression of the Ego-ism which makes modern life so mean, so pitiful, and so wretched."

In spite of these differences of opinion there was much in "The Harbinger" that made it a true successor to "The Dial." A large number of "The Dial" contributors also wrote for "The Harbinger," and the editors of the latter, Ripley and Dwight, were both connected with the former. Another chief contributor to "The Harbinger," Charles A. Dana, also wrote for "The Dial." Other "Dial" writers who wrote more or less frequently for "The Harbinger" were Lowell, Curtis, Cranch, Saxton, W. H. Channing, Ellery Channing, Clarke, and Hedge. Among those who wrote for "The Harbinger" and yet were more or less in sympathy with transcendentalism were T. W. Higginson, Horace Greeley, W. W. Story, John G. Whittier, William F. Channing, and perhaps others.

The full name placed at the head of the associationist journal was "The Harbinger, devoted to Social and Political Progress. Published by the Brook Farm Phalanx." The motto of the paper was this sentence: "All things at the present day stand provided and prepared, and await the light." "The Harbinger" was a weekly of sixteen three-column pages, and its day of publication was Saturday. The first number appeared on June 14, 1845 ; and the prospectus, which bore that date, clearly defined the purposes of the paper. In politics it proposed to be truly democratic, "cherishing the deepest interest in the advancement and happiness of the masses." Independent in relation to parties, it held itself ready to criticise all alike when they failed to work for the interests of the people. Its chief object, however, was to advance "the cause of a radical, organic social reform as essential to the highest development of man's nature." It also proposed to advocate "the principles of universal unity" set forth by Charles Fourier, "to discuss and defend these principles without any sectarian bigotry, and in the catholic and comprehensive spirit of their great discoverer. The social reform, of whose advent the signs are everywhere visible, comprehends all others ; and in laboring for its speedy accomplishment we are conscious that we are devoting our best ability to the removal of oppression and injustice among men, to the complete emancipation of the enslaved, to the promotion of genuine temperance, and to the elevation of the toiling and down-trodden masses to the inborn rights of humanity."

"The Harbinger" had a decided literary flavor, and of such a quality as to connect it intimately with "The Dial." Its literary ability was of a high order, many of its essays and editorials being not only able but finely written. It published much excellent poetry, and by some of the leading poets of the day. In its pages first appeared "Consuelo" in this country, translated by Francis George Shaw, one of the stanchest friends and supporters of Brook Farm, who lived in its immediate vicinity, but never became a member of the community. It is of interest, therefore, that the prospectus of "The Harbinger" defined its relations to literature in much the same spirit that characterized "The Dial": "In literature, 'The Harbinger' will exercise a firm and impartial criticism without respect of persons or parties. It will be made a vehicle for the freest thought, though not of random speculations; and with a generous appreciation of the various forms of truth and beauty, it will not fail to expose such instances of false sentiment, perverted taste, and erroneous opinion as may tend to vitiate the public mind or degrade the individual character. Nor will the literary department of 'The Harbinger' be limited to criticism alone. It will receive contributions from various pens, in different spheres of thought; and, free from dogmatic exclusiveness, will accept all that in any way indicates the unity of Man with Man, with Nature, and with God. Consequently, all true science, all poetry and arts, all sincere literature, all wise analysis of mind and character will come within its province."

It will be seen by this statement of its purposes that "The Harbinger" was by no means a repetition of "The Dial," with an associationist attachment; but that it was more critical of social wrongs, more aggressive, and with a distinct mission proposed for itself. The last paragraph of the prospectus might have appeared in "The Dial" as clearly defining its own spirit, showing that the two journals were aiming at the same thing by different methods: "We appeal for aid in our enterprise to the earnest and hopeful spirits in all classes of society. We appeal to all who, suffering from a resistless discontent in the present order of things, with faith in man and trust in God, are striving for the establishment of universal justice, harmony, and love. We appeal to the thoughtful, the aspiring, the generous everywhere, who wish to see the reign of heavenly truth triumphantly supplanting the infernal discords and falsehoods on which modern society is built, for their sympathy, friendship, and practical co-ope-ration in the undertaking which we announce to-day."

With the number for October 30, 1847, "The Harbinger"

ceased to be published at Brook Farm, and on November 6 its publication began in New York in different form and with a great change in its contents. The editors were Parke Godwin, Charles A. Dana, and George Ripley, with W. H. Channing and John S. Dwight as the Boston editorial writers. But the associationist movement was waning when the paper made this removal, and it continued to exist only until February 10, 1849, which was the date of the last number. "The Harbinger" was succeeded by "The Spirit of the Age," edited by W. H. Channing, which was published in New York as a weekly from July 7, 1849, to April 27, 1850. "It was rich in thought and expression," says O. B. Frothingam, "affluent in sentiment, various in discussion. Its tone was Christian, after Mr. Channing's well-known conception of the gospel." Another attempt to continue "The Harbinger" was made in Boston by John S. Dwight. Beginning with August 30, 1849, he edited a department in the "Daily Chronotype" of that city, edited and published by Elizur Wright; but this arrangement continued only for a few months. In this attempt Dwight secured the assistance of W. H. Channing, W. F. Channing, Dana, Brisbane, Cranch, and others connected with Brook Farm and the associationist movement. These journalistic efforts failed because association had had its day, and new interests were coming forward that turned the minds of the people in other directions.

"The Massachusetts Quarterly Review" was published in Boston from December, 1847, to September, 1850. The editors were Emerson, Parker, and J. Elliot Cabot, all of them contributors to "The Dial." It was projected by Theodore Parker and Dr. Samuel G. Howe, in order that the men of more liberal opinions, and those interested in radical reforms, might have an opportunity of expressing themselves. Concerning the origin of this review Mr. Cabot has given the inside history . "There were meetings at Emerson's house looking to a new quarterly review which should be more alive than was the 'North American' to the questions of the day. Parker and Howe were the persons most forward in the matter. Mr. Sumner came up and spoke approvingly of the undertaking, but doubted whether the time was quite ripe for it. Thoreau was there, but contented himself with asking whether any one present found difficulty in publishing in the existing journals anything that he might have occasion to say. On the whole but little zeal was manifested, nor would anybody promise definite contributions. But it was taken for granted that the new review was to be; the main discussion was about the editor. Mr. Parker wished to put Emerson forward, but Emerson declined; other persons were talked of, but nothing was distinctly agreed upon that I remember, except a committee, consisting of Emerson, Parker, and Howe, for the drafting of a manifesto to the public. This Emerson wrote, and he seems to have supposed his office thereby discharged. But when the first number reached him in England, he found himself set down, with Parker and me, 'assisted by several other gentlemen,' as editors. He did not like this, but suffered his name to stand until, after his return home, the fourth number appeared with the announcement that he would now 'of course' contribute regularly. Then he insisted upon withdrawing, and Parker became, what in fact he had always been, sole editor."

A paragraph or two from the address to the public will give Emerson's idea of what the new review was to be, as well as his conception of what the time demanded in the way of honest convictions and plain-spoken words. "A journal that would meet the real wants of this time," he wrote, "must have a courage and power sufficient to solve the problems which the great groping society around us, stupid with perplexity, is dumbly exploring. Let it not show its astuteness by dodging each difficult question, and arguing diffusely every point on which men are long ago unanimous. Can it front this matter of socialism, to which the names of Owen and Fourier have attached, and dispose of that question? Will it cope with the allied questions of government, non-resistance, and all that belongs under that category? Will it measure itself with the chapter of slavery, in some sort the special enigma of the time, as it has provoked against it a sort of inspiration and enthusiasm singular in modern history? There are literary and philosophical reputations to settle. The name of Swedenborg has in this very time acquired new honors; and the current year has witnessed the appearance, in their first English translation, of his manuscripts. Here is an unsettled account in the book of fame; a nebula to dim eyes, but which great telescopes may yet resolve into a magnificent system. Here is the standing problem of Natural Science, and the merits of her great interpreters, to be determined; the encyclopedical Humboldt and the intrepid generalizations collected by the author of the ' Vestiges of Creation.'

"What will easily seem to many a far higher question than any other is that which respects the embodying of the conscience of the period. Is the age we live in unfriendly to the highest powers, to that blending of the affections with the poetic faculty which has distinguished the religious ages? We have a better opinion of the economy of nature than to fear that those varying phases which humanity presents will ever leave out any of the grand springs of human action. Mankind, for the moment, seem to be in search of a religion. The Jewish cultus is declining; the divine, or as some will say, the truly human, hovers, now seen, now unseen, before us. This period of peace, this hour when the jangling of contending churches is hushing or hushed, will seem only the more propitious to those who believe that man need not fear the want of religion, because they know his religious constitution, — that he must rest on the moral and

religious sentiments, as the motion of bodies rests on geom-
etry. In the rapid decay of what was called religion, timid
and unthinking people fancy a decay of the hope of man.
But the moral and religious sentiments meet us everywhere,
alike in markets as in churches. A God starts up behind
cotton-bales also. The conscience of man is regenerated as
is the atmosphere, so that society cannot be debauched.
That health which we call Virtue is an equipoise which
easily redresses itself, and resembles those rocking-stones
which a child's finger can move and a weight of many
hundred tons cannot overthrow."

The review did not prove to be as good as this statement
of its purposes, Emerson's only contribution to its pages.
Among its writers were Lowell, Henry James, Richard Hil-
dreth, Wendell Phillips, and John Weiss. Parker was the
chief contributor, as well as the editor. He wrote to a
friend that "we want a tremendous journal, with ability
in its arms and piety in its heart." To Charles Sumner he
wrote: "If there were such a journal, ably conducted, it
would have two good influences: 1. It would strike a salu-
tary terror into all the Ultramontanists and make them see
that they did not live in the Middle Ages — that they are
not to be let alone dreaming of the garden of Eden, but are
to buckle up and work; 2. It would spread abroad the
ideas which now wait to be organized, some in letters, some
in art, some in institutions and practical life."

The circulation of this review must have been small,
though Parker said it paid its way, and that it was discontinued because of the failure of the publishers. The contributors were few and voluntary, and therefore were not
paid, or inadequately. Many of Parker's ablest papers and
reviews appeared in its pages, and he gave to it zealous and
faithful labor. "The Massachusetts Quarterly Review," although in a real sense a successor to "The Dial," was of
quite another quality, and its flavor was very different. It

was more polemical, reformatory, and aggressive. It was less literary, poetical, and transcendental. It was a review of the conventional type, with learned and heavy articles; and it was critical, as well as aggressive. Parker said it was " The Dial " " with a beard ; " but it was far other than that, for the one could not have grown into the other.

In 1849 Miss Elizabeth Peabody appeared as the editor and publisher of " Æsthetic Papers," one number only of which was published. It was to be of the same form, size, and type as " The British and Foreign Review," and a number was to " appear whenever a sufficient quantity of valuable matter shall have accumulated to fill 256 pages. This will in no case happen more than three times a year, perhaps not oftener than once a year." The prospectus announced : " The terms of patronage proposed are peculiar to itself. No person is asked to subscribe for more than one number in advance ; but whoever is so far pleased with the current number as to desire another is requested to send an order to that effect to the Editor. When a sufficient number of orders are given to pay for the publication, including compensation to the authors, a new number will be printed ; the Editor being content to receive such profit as may accrue from the sale of other numbers not subscribed for beforehand." This method of publication was not successful, as ought to have been anticipated ; and only fifty subscriptions were secured.

The purpose of the " Æsthetic Papers " was admirable, as stated in the prospectus : " The Editor wishes to assemble upon the high æsthetic ground (away from the regions of strife, in any bad sense) writers of different schools, — that the antagonistic views of philosophy, of individual and social culture, which prevail among the various divisions of the church, and of the scientific and literary world, may be brought together, and a white radiance of love and wisdom be evolved from the union of the many-colored rays, that shall cultivate an harmonious intellectual and moral life in our country. Individuals of all parties have already expressed, by letters and in conversation, their interest in this plan; and the Editor hopes another number may present a practical exemplification of the fact that all believe that on the æsthetic ground all may meet." In the introductory article the editor discussed the meaning of the word " æsthetic," and she said : "It is the watchword of a whole revolution in culture. Like Whig and Tory, it is the standard of a party; it marks the progress of an idea. It is as a watchword we use it, to designate, in our department, that phase in human progress which subordinates the individual to the general, that he may reappear on a higher plane of individuality."

The table of contents of the " Æsthetic Papers," which appeared with no date but the year of publication, and with no number or volume, was a remarkable one. Following the introductory paper on " Æsthetics " by the editor, the titles and writers were as follows : "Criticism," by Samuel G. Ward; "Music," John S. Dwight; "War," R. Waldo Emerson; "Organization," Parke Godwin; "Genius," Sampson Reed; "The Dorian Measure," with a Modern Application, the editor; "Crawford's Orpheus," the editor; "A Spirit's Reply;" "Correspondence," J. J. G. Wilkinson; "Mainstreet," N. Hawthorne; "Abuse of Representative Government," S. H. Perkins; "Resistance to Civil Government, a Lecture delivered in 1847," H. D. Thoreau; "Hymn of a Spirit Shrouded," Ellen Sturgis Hooper; "The Meditations of a Widow;" "Language," the editor; "Vegetation about Salem, Mass.," An English Resident; "The Twofold Being," Thomas Wentworth Higginson; "The Favorite," Louisa S. Higginson [sister of T. W. H.].

Six of the contributors to the "Æsthetic Papers" had written for "The Dial;" and it may be regarded as in a considerable degree a continuation of that journal. The transcendental flavor was preserved, and if an element of æsthetic appreciation appeared, it influenced no one but the editor to any considerable extent. The plan of this publication, however, was an admirable one, and it ought to have succeeded for the sake of the influence it might have exerted in giving American literature and life a more æsthetic character.

During the year 1860 Moncure D. Conway, then the minister of the Unitarian church in Cincinnati, published in that city " The Dial: A Monthly Magazine for Literature, Philosophy and Religion." It began with January of that year and ended with December, there being published twelve numbers of sixty-four pages each, the subscription price being two dollars. Though Conway made no reference to the original " Dial," yet his magazine was evidently named after it. In " A Word to Our Readers," with which the first number opened, the purpose of the magazine was distinctly set forth : " Only that which lives can impart life. And the magazine which we now introduce to our countrymen cannot live but by the life it can supply. Such reciprocal vitality, we believe, must depend on the degree in which it shall be representative of the Spirit of the Age — a phrase which we fear is too commonplace to carry with it always its deep purport. What can the spirit of the age mean but that leading tendency, co-ordinating all interests, which gives to that age an individual character and a special strength ? . . .

" There was a period when the Roman Catholic Church represented that which was deepest, most immortal in the masses of men. . . . In course of time Protestantism became in turn a tradition rather than a conviction ; a thing borne with sufferance, not with joy. As a conviction it culminated in the planting of New England ; then its spirit began a slow ebb. Then rose up the prophets of a new faith and hope ; and Channing, Freeman, Hollis, the Wares, the Buckminsters, easily gained the throne of American thought.

195

After them came a period of theological empiricism, confusing a specific and temporary movement with the eternal and progressive spirit on which the Unitarian movement was but another bead strung. Again was the witness borne, and the command forward heard. But the prophets were stoned, the Lord at his coming denied. With what result? He who looks for Boston Unitarianism will see a series of stranded churches — churches once alive, now disintegrated, sold at auction to other sects, here and there a fusion of two or three in one to preserve even the name that they live, pastors leaving them for the fleshpots of orthodoxy, vainly crying to heaven or beyond the sea for shepherds. . . .

" Has the spirit which convinces the world, which conquers human hearts, filling them with a courage and hope which have no suspense, left the world? Surely, it must take some conviction to build up on half a continent free schools and colleges as grand as the old cathedrals. Surely, it must be a somewhat active spirit which in a few years has multiplied a few anti-slavery men, holding heated conferences in garrets, into two million of open lovers of and voters for freedom. And must it not have been something else than a suspense of faith which, in less than fifteen years has raised up twenty-seven ministers, and more than as many thousand of laity, to stand boldly where in 1845 Theodore Parker and his congregation stood alone in the United States? It is a law that nothing is ever superseded but by something better; and our eyes have no tears for the old blossoms which are falling, because they are fixed on the swelling fruits for which they make way. . . .

" ' The Dial' stands before you, readers, a legitimation of the Spirit of the Age, which aspires to be free: free in thought, doubt, utterance, love, and knowledge. It is, in our minds, symbolized not so much by the sun-clock in the yard, as by the floral dial of Linnæus, which recorded the advancing day by the opening of some flowers and the closing of others; it would report the Day of God as recorded in the unfolding of higher life and thought, and the closing up of old superstitions and evils ; it would be a Dial measuring time by growth."

The names of the contributors to this magazine were not often given, but among them were Emerson, W. H. Furness, C. T. Brooks, and Joel Benton. Under the title of "The Catholic Chapter" it gave selections from Confucius, the "Laws of Menu," Plato's "Phædo," Alcott's "Orphic Sayings," and James Martineau. This magazine was of the radical Unitarian type in theology, and it was outspoken on all subjects it touched. The parting word printed in the last number said that "the principle of the supremacy of reason" was that which the magazine represented. "It is for the right to think, and not be merely tolerated, or not burnt that rationalism has been contending." "In the broad principle of reason we have the vital power which can unite both wings of the church [Unitarian] in one body of saving power; and when Liberal Christianity shall rise on these pinions we are sure that it will pass over the continent with healing in its wings." In spite of the announcement of the discontinuance of the magazine a proposition was printed on the cover to continue it as a quarterly, with contributions from Emerson, Frothingham, Furness, Howells, Joel and Myron Benton, the ex-abbé Miel, Sanborn, and others. Nothing came of this proposition, however.

In September, 1865, was begun in Boston the publication of "The Radical," which represented the transcendentalism of this later date. Its editor was Sidney H. Morse, who was aided by Joseph B. Marvin in the third, fourth, and fifth volumes. Morse was an ardent transcendentalist, and a sculptor of eminence, his busts of Emerson, Parker, and others of his friends, being well known and much admired. Of the contributors to its pages, only A. B. Alcott, Elizabeth P. Peabody, and Charles T. Brooks had written for "The

Dial." Alcott furnished it with a considerable part of what now appears in his "Tablets," and many short sketches of philosophers who were transcendentalists or mystics. Among the other contributors were David A. Wasson, John Weiss, O. B. Frothingham, Moncure D. Conway, William J. Potter, Cyrus A. Bartol, George Howison, T. W. Higginson, Samuel Longfellow, George S. Burleigh, W. J. Linton, B. W. Ball, Richard J. Hinton, Edward Rowland Sill, Ednah D. Cheney, and Samuel Johnson. "The Radical" was ably conducted, and it contained many poems and essays of ability. It was more aggressive than "The Dial," and contained much more in the way of theological discussion. In fact, its publication was begun to represent the interests of the Free Religious Association, with which most of its contributors were connected. The more aggressive phase of this movement was represented by "The Index," the publication of which began in Toledo, Ohio, January 1, 1870, and which removed to Boston at the beginning of September, 1873. In this weekly journal, although representing the same interests as "The Radical," and contributed to by the same persons to a large extent, transcendentalism found less favor. Polemical scientific views had come to take its place, with the result that the idealists gradually withdrew from its support.

No attempt can be made here to continue the history of transcendentalism in New England to the present time, though it is a most inviting theme. Some of its later phases were represented by the Radical Club, or the Chestnut Street Club, which met in the parlors of Rev. and Mrs. John T. Sargent, from the spring of 1867 to the winter of 1880–81. Other phases were represented by the Parker Fraternity Lectures of the same period, which attracted wide attention. These lectures gave the best that transcendentalism had to utter, and drew large audiences. Still another phase was the organization of the Free Religious Association, which was planned at a meeting held in the house of Dr. Cyrus A. Bartol, February 5, 1867. An organization was perfected at a meeting held in Horticultural Hall, Boston, May 30, 1867, the objects being " to promote the interests of pure religion, to encourage the scientific study of theology, and to increase fellowship in the spirit." Among the speakers at this meeting were Emerson, Higginson, Frothingham, Lucretia Mott, John Weiss, Robert Dale Owen, Wasson, Oliver Johnson, and Francis E. Abbot.

The growth of transcendentalism, however, has not been confined to these Boston meetings and organizations; but it has spread throughout the country, and into all churches. It has no organization that now represents it, and no journal is published in its name. Outwardly it seems to have been a failure, and to have disappeared; but it has been a leaven everywhere, and all the more so since it has ceased to have any visible form or representatives. This is fully in harmony with its spirit and intent, which require that it shall be inward and vital in its effects. No church stands for it, and therefore it is a power in all churches. As a creed it is forgotten, but as a spiritual life it was never so active and effective as now.

END OF VOL. I.